PORTER, H. BOONE
KEEPING THE CHURCH YEAR

DATE DUE

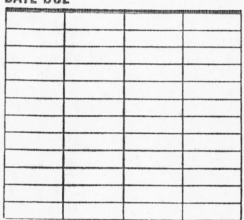

WORSHIP LITURGY

DEMCO

Harry Boone Porter, Jr.

Keeping the Church Year

A Crossroad Book

The Seabury Press / *New York*

1977
The Seabury Press
815 Second Avenue
New York, N.Y. 10017

Library of Congress Cataloging in Publication Data

Porter, Harry Boone.
  Keeping the church year.
Originally published in a monthly column in the magazine The Living church.
Includes index.
1. Church year—Addresses, essays, lectures.   I. The Living church.
II. Title.
BV30.P67   263'.9   77-13338   ISBN 0-8164-2161-7

Printed in the United States of America

ALLELUIA
CHRIST OUR PASSOVER IS SACRIFICED FOR US
✝
THEREFORE LET US KEEP THE FEAST
ALLELUIA

Contents

Preface

    The feasts and special seasons of the Christian calendar come to us year after year. Sometimes they bring excitement, joy, and deep spiritual perceptions. At other times they bring frustration, puzzlement, or mere disregard. The Christian year, like any year, has to be lived and experienced in order to have reality. Religious festivals have little meaning for those who simply observe them as passive spectators. The ideas and suggestions in this book are intended to open many doors for active participation by all sorts of people in the liturgy of the Church.

    The observance of the Christian year has been a major concern in the study and renewal of worship. Greater emphasis on distinctive seasons and important feasts has been characteristic of the liturgical movement of the twentieth century. A major achievement of this movement has been to provide for a fuller observance of Holy Week and Easter, and to restore, in modified form, the dramatic ancient rites and ceremonies for these solemn days. Such provisions for special times of the year constitute one of the distinctive characteristics of the Proposed Book of Common Prayer in the Episcopal Church. This present collection of essays is extended to help clergy and lay people explore these new possibilities and utilize them, in their own local parishes, in constructive and helpful ways. Some of the ideas offered here are very simple. Others are more elaborate. All have been found workable, however, in ordinary parish situations, utilizing the resources and talents of ordinary people.

    Those talents are there! One of the great rewards of liturgical renewal in a congregation is to see these talents come to the surface, to see the volunteers coming forward, to see new ideas being suggested and new results emerging. The opportunity to express oneself in words, in songs, in silence, with colors or symbols, or through sacred actions, is precious. The church is one of the few places where people can gather to sing, to voice their deepest feelings, and to celebrate and solemnize the most profound meanings of life and death. To share in this is a sacred privilege.

It is hoped that these pages will be of practical use not only to clergy but to organists and directors of choirs, lay readers, teachers, members of altar guilds and sacristans, those who train acolytes and servers—all who take part in planning and arranging services of worship. It is hoped that the man or woman in the pew will also find new understanding and insight here. It is anticipated that these essays will be of particular help to parish liturgy committees as they assume a responsible and creative role in stimulating and developing the life of worship in their congregations. This book has been planned specifically to meet the needs of members of the Episcopal Church, but it is sincerely hoped that members of other Churches will find useful material here also. The author is indebted to friends in other Churches for a number of the ideas being presented. All readers should understand that this is primarily a collection of essays on particular days and seasons; it is in no sense a systematic commentary on the Church Year as a whole.

This material was originally published in a monthly column entitled "Feasts, Fasts, and Ferias," which has appeared since May, 1974, in the magazine *The Living Church.* The author is grateful to the now retired editor, the Rev. Carroll E. Simcox, Ph.D., and to many readers who have offered suggestions, questions, and encouragement, and to those who, in a number of instances, have urged that steps be taken to publish the articles in a more permanent form. Such publication has required considerable revision and reorganization of the material. In the original column, some things needed to be repeated each year at certain seasons but do not need to be stated more than once in a book. In other cases, essays dealt with particular juxtapositions of dates that rarely occur, and of course the sequence of thought from month to month had to be adapted to the arrangement of a book. It is hoped, however, that no material of permanent value has been omitted. The Index will assist readers in locating specific items which may have been transferred from an earlier context. Another factor in the revision of the material has been the widespread consensus within the Episcopal Church as to the future use of the Proposed Book of Common Prayer. At the request of the publisher, this edition of the Prayer Book has been adopted as the basis for all specific references to prayers, chants, and rubrics.

I am grateful to my wife, Violet M. Porter, for many suggestions embodied in the original articles, and for her assistance in revising them. I am indebted to the Rev. Lewis W. Towler of the Diocese of Michigan for ideas in Essay 18, to the Rev. Thomas B. Woodward of the Diocese of Rochester for ideas in Essay 31, and to the Very Rev. J. C. Michael Allen of the Diocese of Missouri in regard to Essay 35. I wish to thank Captain Howard Galley, C.A., of the Seabury Press for many editorial suggestions.

Lastly, I wish to express my appreciation to the many persons who have attended conferences, workships, and meetings relating to the observance of the Church Year at Roanridge Training and Conference Center in Kansas City during the past seven years. These have included members and consultants of the Standing Liturgical Commission, members of diocesan and parish committees and commissions, members of the Associated Parishes, and interested clergy and lay people from many backgrounds. An annual workship on the observance of Lent and Easter, and the yearly celebration of the Great Vigil of the Resurrection, have been especially valuable. Participants in these and many other events have contributed much both to these pages and to the pages of the Proposed Book of Common Prayer.

Roanridge
Eastertide, 1977 *H. Boone Porter, Jr.*

I

Advent

Red Letter Days

All Saints — concludes church year
as soon as Feasts are over

I:
Preparing for Advent

The ending of the Church Year has many harbingers. Already in the beginning of November, All Saints' Day has dramatically concluded the past year's cycle of red letter feasts. Next year's cycle will begin with St. Andrew's Day which is always just before or after Advent Sunday. Although it is not part of the traditional Anglican calendar, the American Thanksgiving fittingly symbolizes the conclusion of the agricultural year. Meanwhile, in most parts of the United States, the falling of the last leaves from the trees, the wilting of the last flowers in the garden, and the dry stalks and stems along the roadside, all speak to us of a year coming to a close, which, in turn, speaks to us of the mortality of all things. It was in this vein that our great contemporary poet, T. S. Eliot, wrote

> Where is there an end of it, the soundless wailing,
> The silent withering of autumn flowers
> Dropping their petals and remaining motionless;
> Where is there an end to the drifting wreckage,
> The prayer of the bone on the beach . . .

(The Dry Salvages II)

Christian theologians have asserted that the Christian Year is based on the historical events of salvation, not on the fertility cycle of nature. This is an important but only partial truth. We do celebrate the historical events, but it is the cycle of nature which in various ways (in various climates) builds up much of the emotional force of these Christian observances. Conversely, for many urbanized people today, the Church Year is one of their few remaining conscious links with the seedtime and harvest of the natural world. It is again the highly urbanized T. S. Eliot who reminds us that our humanness requires such links with the earth,

> Which is already flesh, fur and faeces,
> Bone of man and beast, cornstalk and leaf.

(East Coker I)

During the final weeks of the old Church Year, some parishes go right on having the altar decorated week after week with various elegant combinations of greenhouse flowers. This is a lost opportunity to express the reality of the fall. While they are available, sprays of autumn leaves are very appropriate decorations. Later on, interesting and attractive bouquets can be made of plant stalks, clusters of berries, and other November materials. There are many creative possibilities for altar guilds to work on. The last Sunday before Advent is somewhat different. With the new lectionary, this Sunday lends itself to white vestments, and bright colored flowers are certainly fitting then. During Advent, it is not necessary to have any flowers on the altar. Four weeks of austerity and simplicity in the decoration of the church will give greater impact to the wealth of decoration which will appear at Christmas.

Autumn is the time to make other plans about the Advent liturgy. It is, first of all, a season to recall the Old Testament preparation for the coming of the Messiah. Churches that do not normally use an Old Testament lesson in the Eucharist should certainly consider the desirability of doing so for these four weeks. The lessons provided for the Sundays of Advent in the new lectionary are certainly good.

In Advent the canticle *Benedictus,* with its references to St. John the Baptist, certainly should be used, either in Morning Prayer, or after one of the readings at the Eucharist. It is cause for regret that in some parishes this canticle has been neglected for many years. If it is sung every Sunday at the late service in Advent, the congregation will easily regain the ability to sing it: it can also be said at the early services on these days. It should, of course, be explained to the congregation in clear and simple terms why this canticle is especially appropriate in Advent.

Another traditional Anglican formulary for Advent is the Litany. It may be used either as the conclusion of Morning or Evening Prayer, or as the introduction to the Eucharist. If the Great Litany is used with either Rite One or Rite Two for the Holy Eucharist in the Proposed Book of Common Prayer, the rubric near the top of page 406 permits it to fit conveniently with the first part of the service. The Prayers of the People which usually follow the Creed may then be appropriately omitted, as the Great Litany will have covered all the principal topics of intercession.

What is said above about flowers also applies to the *Gloria in excelsis*. We omit it in Advent to give a change of tone, a more austere mood, to the liturgy. After four weeks of disuse, this great chant will have renewed impact when we join the angels in singing it again at Christmas in honor of the Savior who came to us as a baby in a stable.

2:
The Evening of the Year

The days are getting notably shorter. Once more sunset twilight, and the coming of darkness are a more conscious part our daily life. In traditional Christian piety, the darkness of evening is especially associated with the season of Advent. The coming of night communicates to us, as no mere words ever can, the transitory quality of life, the futility of so much human busy activity, and the mysteriousness of God's ultimate purposes.

If your parish church wishes a more effective and vivid observance of the season of Advent, then a good question to ask is: What sort of evening services do you have? Many parishes nowadays find that evening is the only time on the weekdays when a service can be planned for any considerable number of people. For many people, early evening is the only really free time of day. In any event, evening services should not be noisy or bustling affairs. Evening is for shadows, candles, singing, and periods of quiet. In the Proposed Prayer Book, An Order of Worship for the Evening offers a number of suggestions. These are applicable to any sort of evening service: Eucharist, office, some rite such as the Great Litany, parts of the catechism, or other observance.

The option of having the Eucharist in the evening merits special consideration. Important as the "Lord's own service" is, it should not be the only form of corporate worship provided on weekdays. Also, a Sunday evening service may be envisaged as an additional devotion for people who have already been to the Eucharist in the morning. (Yes, there are people who sometimes like to go to church twice!) In these cases, the evening service should be quite different in form and manner from the Eucharist.

On the other hand, when the Eucharist is in the evening, it may well incorporate some features of an evening office. At the beginning, when the candles are lit at the altar, the ancient lamp-lighting hymn *Phos hilaron* may be sung. (We have two versions in the Hymnal, Hymns 173 and 176. It is hoped we may someday learn to chant the new translation given on pages 64, 112, 118, and 139 of the new Prayer Book.) The *Magnificat* can be used between the Epistle and Gospel, and few will not welcome the *Nunc dimittis* at the conclusion.

In choosing hymns for an evening service, one should not succumb to the temptation of using all the old "bedtime hymns." After all, no one is going to bed just yet. Evening hymns should acclaim and recognize the presence of God during an important sector of our daily life. This is why the ancient lamp-lighting hymn is especially good at the beginning. Hymn 181 is notable for its recognition that darkness is beautiful—after all, this is what really underlies the evening office. For evenings in Advent, what the Hymnal offers is truly fantastic. Hymn 3 (Wake, awake) is one of the greatest ever written. Hymns 4, 8, and 11 are all very suitable for evening. As for Hymn 6, it is worth an evening service just to sing this in a half-darkened church. With the Order of Worship for Evening, lessons may be chosen with special suitability for the services at which these hymns are sung. The Parable of the Wise and Foolish Virgins, St. Matthew 25:1–13, is extremely powerful in an evening service in which Hymn 3 is sung.

Advent, the evening of the year, prepares us for Christmas. It also prepares us for the final end of human history and for death. No one has expressed this feeling more eloquently than the great seventeenth-century bishop, Lancelot Andrewes. He was one of the translators of the Authorized Version of the Bible and was a great advocate both of public liturgical worship and of private devotion. Look him up in the new *Lesser Feasts and Fasts* (revised edition, 1973, Church Hymnal Corporation), page 179. In his famous *Preces Privatae* ("Private Prayers") he wrote:

Gotten past the day
I give Thee thanks, o Lord.
The evening draweth nigh:
make it bright.
There is an evening, as of the day,
so also of life:
the evening of life is old age:
old age hath overtaken me:
make it bright . . .

Abide with me, o Lord:
for even now it is towards evening with me,
and the day is far spent
of this travailling life.
Let thy strength be perfected
in my weakness.*

Preces Privatae, F. E. Brightman, trans., Methuen, London, 4th edit.
1949, p. 109.

3:
John the Baptist: Advent Saint

The season of Advent is a grand one for liturgy, with great hymns, stirring biblical passages, and the excitement of the approach of Christmas. The materials used in our services at this season are not, however, a haphazard collection of ingredients. The season of Advent has a distinctive structure which needs to be understood in planning sermons, hymns, and teaching.

Three biblical figures stand out in a special way in the preparation for Christ's coming. First there is Isaiah, the great Old Testament prophet whose book has collected within it so many prophecies of the coming King and Savior. Secondly there is St. John the Baptist, or John the Forerunner, as our Greek friends call him, whose ministry set the stage for that of Jesus. Thirdly, of course, is our Lord's blessed Mother. Each of these three should receive appropriate attention in the liturgy.

In traditional Anglican usage, Isaiah receives great attention in the daily offices in Advent. This continues to be the case in the current revision. Isaiah will now also be read in Old Testament lessons at the Eucharist in some years. In addition, three of the new canticles for Morning Prayer, no. 9, *Ecce, Deus*, no. 10, *Quaerite Dominum*, and no. 11, *Surge, illuminare*, are from Isaiah and are particularly appropriate for Advent.

The Gospels dealing with John the Baptist occur on the second and third Sundays. The fourth Sunday now has a Gospel highlighting St. Mary as the immediate human agent of the Incarnation. This assignment of the final Sunday to our Lord's Mother appears to many as a distinct gain. The new Sunday lectionary involves a three-year cycle, but in all three years, the same sequence of themes is observed in the Advent Gospels.

St. John the Baptist, in both past and present systems of Gospel readings, is of unique importance in the season of Advent. What do we know about him? There are substantially similar passages in Matthew, Mark, and Luke, and somewhat different information in John. There are also some brief references in the Book of Acts. He is not referred to elsewhere in the New Testament, but the Jewish historian Josephus mentions him in contemporary nonbiblical literature. This is a meager record, but enough to give us a fascinating vision of this stern and commanding man.

For many years, John lived in the desert, not the smooth sandy desert of romance but a rough inhospitable terrain of rocky hillsides, cliffs, steep canyons, and arid plains. It was much like the scenery familiar to us from cowboy movies, a lonely area inhabited, if at all, by bandits, wolves, and an occasional lion. It was a land scorched by the sun in the daytime and chilled at night under the vast sky. Here was the place where this John, like Old Testament prophets before him and Christian hermits after him, would learn to live with the elements, with himself, and with God. Most of us would not survive three days in such a place. John lived there for years. We do not know how long it was, but it was long enough so that when he returned to human society, he was not like other men. His clothing was odd, and his dedication to health foods was odder. He cared nothing for the rewards, comforts, or honors of this life, and even less for the threats or punishments of worldly power. "There was a man sent from God . . ." (John 1:6). Indeed, here was a man who was a man, for he was truly a man of God.

When such a man spoke, people listened. Even though he addressed his hearers as a brood of vipers, rich and poor alike trudged out to the riverside to hear him preach, and many waded into the muddy waters of the Jordan to have their sins washed away in preparation for the coming of the Messiah. This man certainly merits one or two sermons each year in Advent. His gaunt, ascetic figure stands in striking contrast to the fat man in a red plush suit, which is what we have made of St. Nicholas. John reminds us that Christmas is not primarily about candy, office parties, and new clothes, but is, instead, about the Messiah, who came in judgment as well as in mercy. We will, of course, wish to use Hymns 9 and 10 which specifically celebrate John's message.

Teaching and preaching about the Baptist in Advent, and conveying a sense of how exciting he is, can have an important place in the total strategy of teaching for the year. A feeling for John helps us understand the relation between the Old Testament and the New; it sheds light on the sacrament of baptism, and prepares us for the commemoration of the Baptism of Our Lord in January. It also explains the regular commemoration of John at Morning Prayer in the Song of Zechariah, known as the *Benedictus.*

During the last Sunday of Advent, attention will center on our Lord's Mother. Some of our finest hymns, such as 2, 6, 117, 317, and 477 will be very appropriate. The association of such hymns as 117 and 317 with the Feast of the Annunciation, and the fact that this feast is never observed on a Sunday, has meant that too many Episcopalians never sing them. If 599 is sung, the preacher will have a good opportunity for once to explain what the second stanza means. Since this is one of the most characteristic and best-loved hymns of the Episcopal Church, such an explanation is long overdue in many congregations. For the traditional title of Mary as the Lord's "Bearer," see Definition of Chalcedon, Proposed Prayer Book, page 864.

John and Mary both direct our attention to the physical reality of the Lord's coming in the war-torn Middle East—an area still too often bathed in blood. Pray this Advent for our brothers and sisters there, who need so much the grace of the Prince of Peace.

II

Christmas, Epiphany, and the Lord's Baptism

4:
Getting Ready for Christmas

The newspapers remind us that there are only so many shopping days left before Christmas. We may also recall that there are only so many days left to plan the services of Christmas, to rehearse the music, to decorate the church and do all the other things which have to be done.

In most parishes, the Christmas Eve Eucharist or Midnight Mass will certainly be the best-attended and best-loved service of the year. No doubt many people will be deeply moved by it, even if the music is ill-chosen or the sermon poorly prepared or the decorations in poor taste. Those who are responsible for leading worship, however, should not be seduced by such tolerance. Great feasts should be occasions for raising the standard of quality, not lowering it. People may say (and will say) that they want the service just like the one last year and the year before that and the year before that. Yet people are not likely to return year after year if no new insight, no new vision, no new sense of spiritual reality is communicated to them. The large crowd on Christmas Eve presents a challenging opportunity to communicate the Good News of the Incarnation as effectively as possible. Let us look at some particular items.

Decorating the church with evergreens is fun, and the aroma of coniferous boughs conveys the Christmas spirit in a unique way. In addition, most parishes have various other decorations. In some churches, one sees the entire sanctuary banked with poinsettias. This represents a generous contribution from parishioners, but is it always the best deployment of decorations? So many flowers in the sanctuary often obscure the visibility of the altar and impede the movements of clergy and servers. In many cases, it would be better to put some of these flowers around the pulpit, some around the lectern, some at the font, and some at the side altar, thus marking out the several points of special significance in the building. The sanctuary, furthermore, is not a stage upon which worship is carried out. The entire interior of the church is the space in which worship goes on. Hence, it is theologically, as well as visually, appropriate to distribute decorations, where possible, along the walls or aisles of the nave.

There are also various kinds of original or unique decorations which people may invent and make. Several years ago, for instance, in a very active parish in the Kansas City area, members of the altar guild made three great figures of the Magi which provided an unusual and striking effect for the season. Some parishes are doing things with the idea of St. Nicholas vested as a bishop. All sorts of things can be done with angels—such as large cardboard cut-out figures blowing trumpets and suspended from the ceiling of the church.

Thought should also be given to the officiants. The most experienced and effective lay readers should have the privilege of reading the Old Testament Lesson and the Epistle at the main Christmas services. They should understand the importance of careful practice beforehand. A full church, with people in winter clothes, requires much greater voice projection than a half-empty church. A deacon, if one is available, will of course read the Gospel. It is a time when the rector, and curates, if any, will all wish to be visible. Is there also a retired priest, or a nonparochial priest in your neighborhood? Christmas, like Easter, is an occasion when he might appreciate being invited to vest and serve in the sanctuary. Too much of the time, the priesthood of the Episcopal Church appears in individualistic terms. On great feasts, it is a treat to see several priests standing together at the altar, as fellow ministers of the sacrament of unity.

5:
Midnight Mass

The Midnight Mass of Christmas is a unique occasion, although nowadays in many parishes it is found preferable to have it at 10 P.M. or earlier Christmas Eve. In many places, those who desire a seat must come to church an hour or more before the service, and the choir sings carols during this period. In the hectic rush of the modern American Christmas, such moments of calm are indeed valuable. On the other hand, it is rather unrealistic to suppose that the average person can, without guidance, meditate profitably for an hour. The distribution in the pews of a mimeographed form of devotions in preparation for Christmas Communion may be useful. In some congregations, people welcome reciting Evening Prayer at some point while they are waiting. Ideally, a vigil service of readings from Isaiah and other prophets, alternating with chants and prayers, should precede the Midnight Mass, just as it does the Midnight Mass of Easter. The clergy are understandably reluctant to adopt plans which would have the effect of making the service longer. On the other hand, on Christmas Eve, as on Easter Eve, it is possible to assign certain choral items and some prayers to the vigil instead of to the Eucharist. A homily in the vigil office may cover useful ground and permit the shortening of the subsequent sermon at the Eucharist. These are possibilities to explore.

In many parishes, the most problematical point in the midnight service is at the moment of Communion. Our Victorian Gothic and neo-Colonial churches were, in most cases, not designed for the convenient administration of Holy Communion. Some churches with large staffs have priests or deacons and lay chalice bearers stationed at various points in the building to administer the Sacrament. Often this does not go well, however, and many feel cheated that they cannot approach the altar for Communion. It is generally agreed that at least one of the sacred Elements must be administered by an ordained minister. There will be no final solution to these problems until we engage architects to redesign our chancels and persuade our bishops to ordain many more deacons (at least one for every parish, and several for the large ones).

In the meantime, some useful steps can be taken. In churches where one or more side altars are used as distribution points for the Sacrament, every effort should be made to provide them fully with Christmas decorations, lighted candles, and so forth, so that they will be visually attractive. If possible, ushers should arrange traffic patterns so that those who prefer to get to the high altar may do so. Others will be glad to get to a side altar with less waiting. If, as we would urge, the baptistery is consistently treated as a place of special devotional importance in the church, then people may not be offended at the prospect of receiving Communion there on some occasions.

Finally, not everyone goes to church on Christmas Eve. Some come the next day, and they should not be greeted by a listless liturgy. Even at an early service, a carol or two will be welcomed. (But not *Silent Night* in the morning, please!) So will a brief but well-prepared homily on the Good News of this day.

6:
The Three Epiphanies

The convivial joys of the Twelve Days of Christmas lead on to the Epiphany, or "Twelfth Night," on January 6. Formerly, this was an important holiday in traditional Christian lands. Today it is largely unknown to our American fellow countrymen, who have followed the Scottish custom of observing New Year's Day as the post-Christmas holiday.

Episcopalians have generally been instructed that Christmas commemorates our Lord's birth and the visit of the shepherds, whereas the Epiphany commemorates the visit of the Magi or Wise Men (popularly described as "kings.") The two events are hard to separate, however, and Christmas pageants, crèche scenes, even our own Anglican carols, mix the two together. In ancient Christian tradition, January 6 had "three Epiphanies" associated with it. First is, of course, the visit of the Magi. Second is our Lord's baptism in the Jordan. Third is the first miracle at the wedding feast at Cana as narrated in the second chapter of St. John's Gospel.

When Archbishop Cranmer translated and arranged the English Prayer Book in the sixteenth century, he assigned the account of the baptism to be read at Morning Prayer, the visit of the Magi in the eucharistic Gospel, and the wedding feast at Evensong. This was an ingenious arrangement for an era when the day was a public holiday and many people attended these services. It would scarcely be realistic today, however. Hence our new lectionary continues to have the visit of the Magi on January 6, but also allows this reading on the previous Sunday. This should be useful in parishes where very few worshipers are anticipated on January 6. The second great theme of Epiphany (perhaps the most important theologically), our

Lord's Baptism, will now always be celebrated on the Sunday following Epiphany. The restoration of this commemoration is a matter deserving careful attention on the part of all who are concerned with liturgical planning. Finally, the miracle at Cana will be read in the Gospel on the Second Sunday after Epiphany every third year (Year C in the lectionary), and on the other two years other appropriate passages from the first part of St. John will be read. Each year the themes of all these different days should be thoughtfully considered in advance, and decisions must be made as to the options that exist. It is then possible to assign hymns and carols in a coherent manner, choose sermon topics, and plan suitable decorations and special observances.

It is our long-standing Anglican custom that crèches, Christmas trees, and similar items be removed from the church (and from private homes) following the principal service or services on January 6. This custom deserves to remain in force. The Sunday after Epiphany is a feast, and we will still want white vestments and extra flowers and candles (possibly still some green boughs also), but things specifically pertaining to our Lord's birth and childhood will not be fitting.

7:
The Baptism of Jesus

Our Lord's Baptism by John the Baptist in the Jordan is a major event near the beginning of the Gospel according to SS. Matthew, Mark, and Luke. It is alluded to, less explicitly, in the first chapter of St. John. In ancient liturgical practice, the commemoration of this event was a major observance in the Christian calendar. It continues to be an important and popular celebration among Greeks, Syrians, and other Eastern Christians. Yet it has slipped away from us in the Western Churches. To restore this aspect of the Epiphany observance is an important item in the agenda of liturgical renewal. Episcopalians, and others who are adopting the new three-year lectionary, need to understand, celebrate, and appreciate this observance now assigned to the Sunday after Epiphany.

First of all, like any other feast, this day should be marked out by appropriate decorations, hymns, preaching, prayers, and ceremonies. Before these can be planned, we need to know the meaning and purpose of the occasion. What does the Baptism of Jesus really have to do with your baptism and mine, or the baptism of our children? After all, we are mere sinful humans whereas he was and is the eternal Son of God and the Christ. This is precisely the point. In his baptism, Jesus was declared to be God's Son. When we follow him into the water of the font, we are made sharers of his sonship, we are adopted as his brothers and sisters and hence, through him, adopted as the children of God. Similarly, he was and is the Christ. Uniting ourselves to him in baptism, we are christened, made Christians.

One of the great Anglican writers of the seventeenth century, Bishop Jeremy Taylor, wrote at length of our Lord's Baptism. We may quote one of his many strikingly beautiful paragraphs:

After the holy Jesus was baptized, and had prayed, the heavens opened, the Holy Ghost descended, and a voice from heaven proclaimed him to be the Son of God, and one in whom the Father was well pleased; and the same ointment, that was cast upon the head of our High Priest, went unto his beard, and thence fell to the borders of his garment: for as Christ, our Head, felt these effects in manifestation, so the church believes God does to her, and to her meanest children, in the susception of the holy rite of baptism . . .*

In regard to the decorations of the church, today, as on other feasts, festal vestments and hangings and additional flowers and candles all serve to identify a solemn and joyous day. The special concern today is Holy Baptism. Accordingly, the font and surrounding area can be beautified and made conspicious by flowers and candles and perhaps a banner or other temporary hanging. Many Victorian churches have a stained glass window depicting our Lord's Baptism near the font. In some cases attention can be drawn to such a window on this occasion by putting flowers or candles on the windowsill.

Unfortunately, the question of suitable hymns is not so easily solved. The Hymnal provides two hymns for baptism, 185 and 186; neither is notable for its popularity. Our Lord's Baptism is referred to briefly in the second verse of three hymns: 53, 268, and 344. Are there any others? Hymn 10 ("On Jordan's Bank") has suitability, and 545 ("Hail to the Lord's Anointed") is theologically relevant. It is shocking that not one of our hymns is specifically devoted to our Lord's Baptism and not one well-known major hymn is devoted to the administration of this sacrament. One hopes that some of the new hymns on this theme, or some revived old hymns, will become popular in the years ahead. Among present choices, St. Patrick's Breastplate, Hymn 268, is perhaps the most forceful for this day,

---

*Jeremy Taylor, *The Great Exemplar,* many editions, Addition to Section IX, paragraph 4.

especially if baptisms are to be administered.

As to preaching, there is obviously much to be said. It does not all need to be included in this year's sermon. This feast will be with us for many years to come.

As to special prayers and ceremonies for this day, the best option of all is, of course, to celebrate the sacrament of Holy Baptism with all possible reverence and emphasis. As the public administration of baptism on Sunday morning becomes increasingly the norm throughout the Church, it is obviously desirable not to scatter these at random throughout the year but rather to have groups of people, young and old, baptized together on days of special suitability. The Feast of our Lord's Baptism is precisely such a time, and is so designated in the rubrics of the Proposed Prayer Book, page 312. The idea of having certain special baptismal Sundays is unfamiliar to many of us, and this is an excellent time to introduce the practice.

What if no baptismal candidates are available? Even then it is still possible to express the baptismal nature of the occasion. At the point in the liturgy where the Nicene Creed is usually begun, the priest and servers can go in procession to the font, just as if a baptism were going to occur, perhaps while part of Hymn 268 is being sung. At the font, after suitable words of explanation, the priest leads the congregation in the Renewal of Baptismal Vows, pages 292–294. The use of this material on this day, in place of the usual Nicene Creed, is authorized on page 312. Clergy and servers may then return to the chancel (perhaps while the remainder of Hymn 268 is being sung), and the service may proceed as usual.

8:
Anointed in Christ

One aspect of the sacrament of Holy Baptism to which the Baptism of our Lord calls attention is spiritual anointing or unction (both words mean the same). This is something most English-speaking Christians have missed, but it has a rich background of biblical practice and thought. In the Old Testament, anointing with olive oil was associated with the giving of spiritual power (see, for instance, I Samuel 10:1–12). The Hebrews especially used the ceremony of anointing to consecrate high priests, kings, and prophets (see for example Exodus 30:30; II Samuel 2:4; and I Kings 19:15, 16). The hoped-for Savior of the future was to be anointed by the very Spirit of God (Isaiah 42:1; 61:1) and came to be called the Anointed One, or in Hebrew "Messiah." This was translated into Greek as "Christ," which again means Anointed One. Hence the descent of the Spirit on Jesus at the Jordan has had rich symbolic associations for Christians as a sign of his "christhood." As Bishop Wordsworth wrote in Hymn 53:

> Manifest at Jordan's stream,
> Prophet, Priest, and King supreme

Jesus, however, was to be an unexpected kind of Messiah—his kingship would be expressed on the cross. When we are christened, we receive his mark of the cross. To be his disciple is to to take up the cross and follow him. So we share in his sacrificial ministry as prophet, priest, and king.

Early Christians believed it was important to have an outward and visible expression of anointing in conjunction with this baptismal signing with the cross. So the practice developed of having Christians anointed at the time of baptism with a fragrant oil which was solemnly blessed by the bishop. This oil is usually called _chrism_, a Greek word for ointment, and is related to the word _Christ_. It is applied by the officiating bishop or priest to the forehead of a new Christian in the form of a cross. In many parts of the Christian world, this anointing is regarded as the sacrament of confirmation. It was used almost universally throughout the Christian world from the third century until the sixteenth, and it continues in use among the majority of Christians. Chrism continued to be part of the baptismal rite in the first English Book of Common Prayer of 1549. It subsequently was dropped, although we still speak of children as being "christened." Chrism has remained continuously in Anglican usage only for the anointing of British monarchs at their coronation. Now, however, it is again authorized for use in the Episcopal Church. Because of its biblical basis, its ancient and widespread use, and its rich theological symbolism, many believe its revival to be very desirable.

If the bishop is coming to your parish, and is willing to consecrate holy chrism, we recommend the following procedures: First, obtain pure olive oil from the grocery (very little will be needed). Obtain an aromatic ingredient from a pharmacy, such as synthetic oil of cinnamon or oil of bergamot. It may be necessary to order these a week or more in advance. Purchase the smallest available bottle of it (¼ ounce is adequate). If less familiar aromatic ingredients are to be used, information should be obtained well in advance and orders should be placed several weeks before the material is needed.*When the bishop is to arrive, place a small table covered with a white cloth in the church near the font or in some other suitable place. On a silver or glass tray put a container with about

---

*An aromatic substance of the highest quality, specifically for this purpose, is Bethlehem Chrism Essence, blended and marketed by Dr. Steffen Arctander, R.D. 1, Olyphant, Pennsylvania 18447.

four teaspoons of olive oil in it. For this we suggest a small glass beaker, obtainable from a pharmacy. Also put the little bottle with the aromatic ingredient on the tray (see that the cap is loose before the service) and a small spoon. Provide a paper napkin or two.

If baptism is to be administered, immediately after the blessing of the water, the bishop goes to the table to consecrate the chrism. He should stand back of the table, facing the people, with other clergy to his right and left. A few words of explanation should then be given to the congregation. The bishop may then hold up the beaker of olive oil for all to see it, and with the help of a priest or a deacon, pour the aromatic ingredient into the olive oil. About a spoonful (or the entire contents of a ¼ ounce phial) will be more than adequate. The mixture should be stirred briefly with the spoon. The bishop alone then recites the prayer on page 307 of the new Prayer Book, and the baptismal service continues.

After the administration of the water, the bishop anoints the foreheads of the new Christians, moistening his thumb for this purpose by sticking it into the beaker of chrism—wiping it afterwards with a napkin. After the service the contents of the beaker can be poured into a small bottle with a tight stopper and labeled "Holy Chrism." As chrism is a consecrated sign of the presence of the Holy Spirit in the Church, it should be treated with reverence, and kept in an aumbry, tabernacle, or other safe place. At subsequent baptisms during the year, the officiating priest anoints the foreheads of the newly baptized with it.

If the bishop desires to consecrate chrism on an occasion when baptism is not administered, it is suggested that it be done at a Eucharist celebrated by the bishop with the assistance of other clergy. It may take place right after the sermon (if it has been preached about), or before or after the Offertory. The traditional Western Catholic practice of consecrating the chrism after receiving Holy Communion and before the final prayer of the Eucharist may also be followed. In either case, the bishop may go to the small table, accompanied by other clergy, and follow the same procedure suggested in connection with baptism. Other alternatives are, of course, possible, but we believe the arrangements here suggested can be carried out in the average parish without undue difficulty.

III

The Weeks after Epiphany

9:
Green Sundays

After the festive weeks of Christmas, Epiphany, and the Lord's Baptism, the Church Year resumes a more modest tone. The quieter Sundays of late January, like those of the summer, are familiarly known to many as "Green Sundays." This appellation is of course derived from the green vestments and the green hangings most churches have in the chancel during these weeks, and the green numerals with which ecclesiastical calendars usually designate these Sundays.

Why green? It is often said that green is used in summer because it is the prevailing color of nature, but this explanation is of little help in January or February—certainly not in northern latitudes. This widespread use of green during much of the year is not without merit, for green is indeed a restful color to the eye. On the other hand, it is not an ancient or universal custom. In medieval England, they generally used the finest and newest vestments on great feasts, and the plainer or older ones on ordinary days. Sackcloth was used in Lent. Such an arrangement was eminently sensible. During the seventeenth and eighteenth centuries, colored vestments were rarely used in the Church of England, and no color sequence was followed except that a more austere appearance was normal in Lent. During most of the year, red was commonly used for altar and chancel hangings.

Meanwhile, other parts of the Christian world followed other patterns. Among the Eastern Orthodox Churches, very colorful vestments are used, but generally with no systematic sequence. The exceptions would be a preference in some areas for a dull red during Lent, and among Russians the use of white for all Sundays, since every Sunday celebrates the Resurrection. In France, Italy, and elsewhere, Roman Catholics came to adopt a system of using white, gold, or red for feasts, and violet for penitential times. Green was apparently chosen for the rest of the year as being a pleasant color in between these extremes. For some reason, blue, yellow, and orange, widely used in the Middle Ages, were dropped from the Roman Catholic scheme as major colors, but they continued in use for trimmings and contrasting orphreys. During the late nineteenth and early twentieth centuries, the comparatively modern Roman Catholic system has been widely adopted in Anglican or Episcopal churches, although some of our parishes have followed the less formal English medieval usage. During recent years, both Roman Catholics and Anglicans have been questioning the prevailing system, and artists designing fine vestments have asked for a wider freedom of choice in the use of colored fabrics.

In any case, within the Episcopal Church there are in fact no rubrics or canon laws governing such matters. Colors are generally governed by custom—we normally do what we have been doing, unless there is a good reason to change. Common sense, good taste, and artistic judgment should influence our decision when new vestments are made. Certain churches may have a particular reason for using some special color on many Sundays of the year—for instance, if an unusual color scheme dominates the interior. At the General Theological Seminary in New York, for example, the Victorian Chapel of the Good Shepherd has always presented a difficult problem for the decorator. Several years ago, however, an unusual copper-colored frontal was designed for the altar for use in the ordinary times of the year. The effect has since been widely admired. Some Georgian colonial churches with white woodwork have appropriately revived the eighteenth-century practice of vesting the altar consistently in red. A resort chapel near the sea or a lake might choose to use blue and white as its normal colors. In short, green is not a bad color, but it certainly is not the only option. Meanwhile, the observance of Lent raises other questions to which we must turn in due course.

IO:
To Transfer or Not to Transfer?

During late January and February, as during other parts of the year, there occur certain "red letter days." These are significant feasts, commemorating either events in our Lord's life, or the more important saints—usually saints of the New Testament. The term "red letter" comes from the old custom of printing Church calendars in two colors, using black for lesser feasts and red for the major ones. One will sometimes observe this use of red and black printing in the calendar in some editions of the Book of Common Prayer. The term does not relate to the fact that red vestments are normally used on many of these days.

In most years, these feasts fall on weekdays and unfortunately do not receive the attention they deserve. It is permissible to transfer them to another weekday within the same week, and sometimes it is advantageous to do so. Thus, when a certain red letter day falls on a Monday one year, if a parish has a reasonably well-attended regular mid-week Eucharist on Wednesday or Thursday, it may be desirable to transfer the feast to one of the latter days. Our rubrics do not, however, permit transferring such a feast to a Sunday unless it be the patronal feast of the parish. Thus, in all years when the Feast of the Conversion of St. Paul comes on a weekday, churches dedicated to St. Paul can celebrate the feast on the following Sunday and can make it a major event in the life of the parish. In the infrequent years when the feast falls on Sunday, parishes dedicated to St. Paul would observe it on that Sunday. Other parishes would either transfer the observance to some other convenient day within the week, or they might use some or all of the proper material for the feast on the Sunday, unless it is the last Sunday before Lent.

Parishes dedicated to St. Matthias, on the other hand, find themselves in a different position, since his day, near the end of February, is usually in Lent, and no such feasts can be transferred to or observed on the more solemn Sundays of Lent. The clergy and people of a church dedicated to St. Matthias should choose some other convenient time of year and plan their parish festival then.

Still another situation arises with the Feast of the Presentation of our Lord in the Temple, or the Purification of St. Mary, February 2. In years when this falls on Sunday, it must be so observed. Many churches and institutions named for St. Mary also observe this as their patronal feast. In years when it occurs on a weekday just before Lent, it is appropriately transferred, for a patronal feast, to the preceding Sunday, since it cannot be transferred to a subsequent Sunday within the Lenten season.

All of this seems a bit complicated, but the moral is very clear. Persons who are involved in the planning of worship must look ahead, study the calendar, and consider what options are available. Then they can make constructive choices.

II:
What about Ordinary Days?

In these essays, we necessarily give most of our attention to the major seasons of the Church Year, and to Sundays and other feasts. There remain the ordinary days of the year, the Mondays, Tuesdays, Wednesdays, and so forth, that have no special commemoration or theme connected with them. In traditional ecclesiastical terminology, these are "ferias"—just plain weekdays.

What does the liturgy provide for these normal days which make up most of our lives? In our Anglican tradition, the liturgy provides a great deal for these days—indeed, some of its finest treasures. Daily Morning Prayer (often called Matins) and Daily Evening Prayer (often called Evensong) have for centuries been the best known and most widely admired of Anglican services. Of course, Holy Communion or Mass can be, and often is, celebrated on weekdays, and also there are weddings, funerals, and other services from time to time. Yet the distinctive services specifically intended for daily use are Morning and Evening Prayer. These services are often simply called the "daily offices." They are also known as the "choir offices" because they are led, not from the altar, but from the choir or chancel of the church. They are collectively called the "Divine Office"—a title reflecting the teaching of St. Benedict and others that to engage in the daily round of prayer and praise is, indeed, the "work of God."

The Divine Office also exists in other forms, as in the rites of the Eastern Orthodox Church, and in the daily services contained in the Roman Catholic breviary. Certain communities of monks and nuns have their own arrangements of offices occurring at intervals during the day. Many Episcopalians are familiar with certain shorter traditional offices which may be used as optional supplements to Morning and Evening Prayer, such as the midday office and Compline at bedtime. All of these traditions have much in common and make extensive use of the psalms and biblical canticles. The ancient orders for these offices provide a fascinating interplay of different chants, psalms, lessons, and prayers, varying according to the time of the day, the day of the week, and the season of the year. The great achievement of the Anglican office is that it has a very simple basic structure. The most frequently used elements in these services, such as the *Venite,* the *Benedictus,* and the Apostles' Creed, are easily memorized. At intervals between these relatively fixed items, the ever-changing selection of psalms, biblical lessons, and Collects provides a vast amount of variety. Hence, our daily morning and evening services can be easily mastered by anyone who attends them regularly. At the same time, the unending variety of combinations of psalms, lessons, canticles, and prayers constantly opens new windows of spiritual meaning. After ten or twenty years of daily recitation, Matins and Evensong still have new things to say to the worshiper each day. The flexible provisions in the rubrics in the new Prayer Book make it possible to plan the office in ways that are most suitable to local circumstances, with appropriate intercessions, and so forth.

It is ironic that many Episcopalians have little acquaintance with the evening office, and know the morning one only in an elaborate nineteenth-century form at a late hour on Sunday morning. The mystery of the daily offices is the rhythmic beat of praise, Scripture, and prayer interpenetrating ordinary life day after day after day. To discover what this means is one of the great privileges of our Anglican heritage.

Perhaps one of the most urgently needed of all liturgical reforms in the Episcopal Church is precisely a return to daily prayer, and a greater emphasis on the obligation of all Church members to pray daily. It is unlikely that we can have great liturgies on Sundays and feasts if we are out of touch with God on the intervening days. We cannot be fluent in the language of prayer and Scripture if we only speak it one day a week. There are, of course, many ways to pray daily which are legitimate, constructive, and helpful to various people in various circumstances. Yet the Church has distilled its finest and most considered recommendations into the daily office. The best advice the Church has to offer on this subject, the most thoughtfully worked out plans of daily Bible reading, and the most careful balance of joy and penitence, of personal and corporate devotion, are all represented in the Divine Office.

For a parish to fulfill its vocation as an effective local manifestation of Christ's Holy Catholic Church, daily prayer has to have some visible and recognized place in the total parish program and plan of mission and ministry. This topic should be spoken about, preached about, and taught about regularly. People need to be told of the wide range of possible patterns of individual and family prayer which may suit their differing needs and circumstances. Forward Movement and other publishers provide many helpful resources. As has been said, however, the daily office is the best the Church has to offer. Something is seriously lacking if people have no opportunity to learn about it.

Large numbers of very busy clergy find it possible to read the Divine Office daily. There are many lay people, too, who make it a regular part of their life to read at least one office a day. A man may read Morning Prayer on a commuter train in the morning. A housewife may do so at the kitchen table after her family has gotten off. The evening office may be read sitting on the back porch during a few minutes of quiet after the day's work. Others may settle for some selected part of the office. A family, for instance, can say the *Venite*, hear a biblical lesson, and say the Creed, Lord's Prayer, and a morning Collect together at breakfast time.

None of this is very likely to happen if people do not have any opportunity to see the office as a daily reality. Morning Prayer, as we have often seen it on Sunday, is an impressive production involving organist, choir, crucifers, preacher, and so forth. People cannot, and should not, be trying to imitate that in their daily devotions. On the other hand, people are provided with a useful model if they spend an evening at the rectory and read Evening Prayer with the priest and his wife in front of the fireplace. Or a priest may ask anyone in the parish house to join him in saying the morning office in the church or in a side chapel at the beginning of each day's work. In large parishes and Church institutions, the staff can easily arrange to say an office together each day. In some parishes, the lay readers maintain a roster so that two of their number are at an office every day—hence, a consistent schedule can be maintained even if the priest is away or unavoidably detained on certain days. Church conferences and meetings are also good times for people to have the experience of using the office daily, and of singing the canticles. The writer was recently at a conference devoted to the subject of worship. One of the participants, a woman who has a very active and busy life, remarked that she found time to say Morning Prayer daily at home, and she wondered why a religious conference could not find time in its schedule for the same purpose. It is a good question, for it probes the basic priorities of the Church. What does your parish do to enhance and uphold the daily prayers of its members?

12:
Farewell to Alleluia

The last week after Epiphany has a special character, because it marks the conclusion of the use of Alleluia until Easter. The reason for the disuse of Alleluia in Lent is not because it is an evil to be given up, or because we do not wish to praise God in this season, but because in our liturgical tradition Alleluia is associated with Easter in a quite unique way. The full force and beauty of Alleluia is best appreciated at Easter when we have not used it for some weeks previously.

Hence there arose many centuries ago the custom of "burying Alleluia" at the end of the Epiphany season. With the calendar now being adopted in many Churches, the last proper day for the use of Alleluia is Shrove Tuesday, the final day before Lent begins. Monastic communities, theological seminaries, and other churches or institutions which have daily choral services will wish to have this observance on Shrove Tuesday. For most of us, our final singing of Alleluia will be on the Last Sunday after Epiphany.

Our Hymnal provides Hymn 54, "Alleluia, song of gladness," a medieval hymn specifically composed for this observance. Hymn 583, "Sing Alleluia forth in duteous praise," is also a traditional choice. Hymns 347 and 599 are also recommended, and 197 for the eucharistic offertory. These are among our best-loved Anglican hymns which, because of their repeated Alleluias and festive character, are not suitable for Lent. We will resume them with much joy in Easter season when they are appropriate for frequent use. The beautiful custom of saying farewell to Alleluia at the end of the Epiphany season has much to commend it, but like much else, the effect will be largely lost if a few words of explanation are not given to the congregation.

With the new lectionary, this last Sunday before Lent becomes a feast of the glorification of Jesus, virtually a second Feast of the Transfiguration. This event is of great theological significance, and it is a gain to have these additional biblical readings pertaining to it. The hymns which have been recommended are very congenial to the theme of these propers. White vestments are suitable. This will normally* be the last day until Easter that flowers are used on the altar. As we have extra Alleluias, so extra flowers and candles are appropriate at this time.

Why bother about Alleluia? When Archbishop Cranmer produced the first English Prayer Book in the sixteenth century, he simply omitted the word or translated it literally into English as "Praise ye the Lord" (as before the *Venite* at Morning Prayer). Why does the Church retain this term? Alleluia, or its more Hebrew form Hallelujah (see page 584 of new Prayer Book), reasserts itself because it is part of the international, timeless, truly universal language of Christian worship. Like that other Hebrew word *Amen* and the Greek *Kyrie eleison,* it is an expression into which countless generations of worshipers have poured their spiritual feelings and aspirations. It has become a song of the Christian heart, and of the Jewish heart too, to which no mere vernacular phrase can do justice. The ravishing Alleluias of medieval plainsong, the *Hallelujah Chorus* of Handel and innumerable hymns have found in this word the language of the soul. By forgoing it for several weeks, we prepare to return to it with renewed vision and spiritual perception when Easter, the "Feast of Feasts" breaks forth.

Then I heard what seemed to be the voice of a great multitude, like the sound of many waters and like the sound of mighty thunderpeals, crying,

---

*We say "normally" because exceptions are always possible in certain circumstances. If the Feast of the Annunciation (March 25) is the patronal feast of your parish, you will presumably have a fully festal service at that time, even though it is in the midst of Lent.

"Hallelujah! For the Lord our God
the Almighty reigns.
Let us rejoice and exult and give
him the glory,
for the marriage of the Lamb has
come,
and his Bride has made herself
ready."

Revelation 19:6–7

IV

Lent

13:
Expressing the Spirit of Lent

Each year the holy season of Lent comes to us with its call to prayer, almsgiving, and fasting. At this point in human history one hopes that this call will not be regarded as a mere routine, an old custom repeated simply out of habit. Nowadays we ought to see the urgency of prayer for ourselves, our communities, our churches, our nations, and our world. Similarly, the world food crisis raises the question of almsgiving to a level we have never faced before. But what about fasting? It has been out of fashion in recent years. It is evident that the fashion must change. How much food, and what sort of food, each of us should eat is not easily decided by any public agency. Surely the age-old Christian tradition has not been wrong in directing that on at least one day of the week, Friday, people should not normally eat meat. Growing children, lactating mothers, and the sick, can fill up, if they need to, on cheese, eggs, or fish.

Because Lent is so distinctive, and its message so important, the Lenten liturgy has always been different. When the *Gloria in excelsis* is regularly used on Sundays throughout the year in its ancient place at the beginning of the Holy Eucharist, then its omission in Lent establishes a different tone at the start of the service. So, too, with that most familiar word of Christian praise, *Alleluia*. Its omission marks a change of tone. There are a variety of other things that can mark off this season. As in Advent, the Sunday Eucharist may appropriately begin with the Great Litany (see page 5 above), and the usual intercessions after the Creed will in that case be omitted. The Decalogue, or Ten Commandments, may also be used to advantage in this season. A quite workable pattern is to use the Decalogue at the early service, and the Litany at the late service on the first, second, third, and fifth Sundays of Lent. The fourth Sunday is somewhat less penitential in its emphasis (see pages 49–50 below) and the sixth Sunday, Palm Sunday, has its own unique agenda. Another traditional Anglican formulary, which certainly should be used at least once each Lent is the so-called Long Exhortation. The version given on pages 316–317 of the Proposed Book of Common Prayer is excellent, and it says things we all need to hear. Another important feature of the traditional Lenten liturgy is the use of penitential psalms, both in the daily office and in the Eucharist. In the latter, such a psalm is fittingly recited after the Old Testament lesson or after the Epistle.

The spirit and character of a season is conveyed to the eye as well as the ear. In Lent most of our churches adopt vestments and altar hangings of a rich purple trimmed with gold. Some congregations go a step further and have bouquets of purple flowers on the altar. Does purple silk with golden orphreys really suggest repentance and self-denial? At the end of the season, in some parishes crosses, pictures, and statues are veiled—sometimes with see-through lavender gauze. People wonder why crosses are veiled in the season of the cross. Is this the best way to do things?

As with other liturgical questions, looking to the past may present other options. We need not follow the past exactly, but it can open our minds to new possibilities. In Pre-Reformation England, purple was not normally used in Lent. Brocaded silk vestments of all colors were given up. Instead, priests wore chasubles of unbleached linen, suggestive of sackcloth. The same material was used for the altar hangings. If there was a reredos or picture back of the altar, it was covered over with this cloth. Embroidery was not used on these lenten hangings, but symbols of the Passion, such as crosses and crowns of thorns, might be painted or stenciled on it in black, purple, or red. This whole arrangement was called the Lenten array. In Holy Week, in some places, the priest apparently wore a red chasuble—not, one presumes, the festal red silk of Apostles' Days, but rather a modest vestment of dyed linen. The effect is very striking against the pale background of the Lenten array.

In recent years, a number of Episcopal churches have revived or adapted the concept of the Lenten array. Various kinds of off-white or buff-colored fabrics have been used. Suitable designs can be applied to them if desired, with paint, appliqué, or block print.

An attractive frontal for the altar can be made of inexpensive rough cloth, perhaps trimmed with black and red. If desired, a pulpit cloth can be made to match. Candelabra, decorative crosses, pictures, or statues above or behind the altar may be removed or covered over by an expanse of the same cloth. The author is acquainted with one large church the interior of which is heavily dominated by a Victorian stone reredos. A large curtain of burlap was easily constructed to cover it entirely over during Lent. The result was a quiet, clean, restful effect during this season. Such a change of flavor can be welcome.

A number of other things can be done to give a Lenten appearance to a church. At Roanridge, in the small chapel used for daily services, we have usually had a polychromed cross hanging back of the altar, and a matching pair of colorful candlesticks on the altar. In Lent, we have replaced the cross by a rustic one made of two pieces of apple bough, surmounted by a crown of thorns. The usual candlesticks are replaced by a pair of massive wooden ones, finished in natural color, with a band of red around the upper and lower portions. All these things were made without difficulty, it may be mentioned, by local people. They appeared to compare very favorably with the uninteresting brassware so often seen on the altars of Episcopal churches. A small congregation, utilizing the talents of its people, can have furnishings of a very superior quality.

Real crowns of thorns can be used effectively in many ways. If the thorns are large, they convey their meaning in no uncertain terms. To make one, get youngsters to locate a thorn tree in your neighborhood. Cut three-foot lengths of the thinnest, thorniest boughs. They can be made more bendable by soaking them for a day or two in a tub of water. Work them around into a crown and, if desired, tie the boughs permanently together by using thin and scarcely visible green florist's wire, obtainable from a hardware store.

As with other handcrafted artifacts, it is well to get the necessary tools and materials together in advance and proceed to the work in a careful manner. Such a crown can be hung on the front of a pulpit or in some other conspicuous place. At Roanridge we have used a lenten processional cross made from the shaft of a tall straight sapling, with the cross part surmounted by a crown of thorns.

It need hardly be said that supernumerary candlesticks, decorative alms basins, flags, and other such things do not belong in the sanctuary during Lent. They should be kept in the sacristy until Easter.

Lent is a season for repentance, but decorating, or underdecorating, a church for this season can be entertaining. If a number of people in the congregation take part in this project, they will strengthen their own sense of the meaning of the season. When everything is finally in place on Shrove Tuesday evening, all will be able to eat pancakes with satisfaction, ready on the next day to enter, with joy, upon the consideration of those mighty acts whereby God has given to us salvation.

14:
Mid-Lent Sunday

The observance of the season of Lent is supposed to be sufficiently consistent and sufficiently lengthy so that no churchgoer will fail to feel its spirit, or fail to benefit by this time of cleansing, purification, and renewal. On the other hand, it is not supposed to be a time of unmitigated drabness. The Lenten liturgy, thoughtfully performed, has its own movement, interest, and drama. One distinctive point within Lent is the Fourth Sunday, sometimes known as Mid-Lent, Refreshment, or Mothering Sunday.

Ever since medieval times, this has been viewed as a moment of pause in the austerity of the season, a day to remind ourselves that the purpose of Lent is ultimately not sorrow for our sins but the attaining of the glory that is to be revealed. To some extent it marks a change in emphasis between the first part of Lent, when we think mainly of repentance, and the second part of Lent, when our attention shifts to the crucifixion of our Lord.

In the eucharistic lectionary as we have had it in the past, the Gospel has been St. John's account of the miraculous feeding—a story of refreshment in a season of fasting. In the new three-year lectionary, this continues to be read in Year B. In Year A, a similar theme is expressed in the use of Psalm 23. In Year C, we have the story of the first Passover to be eaten in the Promised Land (Joshua 5:9–12). In all three years, there are other passages which speak in other ways of refreshment, renewal, and re-creation.

Mid-Lent Sunday has had curious associations connected with it. In England it was formerly a time to eat "simnel cake," a cake or plum pudding made of "simnel" or fine flour—a special treat during the season of fasting. In a number of Episcopal parishes, some type of large fruitcake is baked prior to this day and is shared at the coffee hour. As is so often the case with such customs, most people have no idea what it is supposed to signify, and a brief explanation would be welcome.

The old term, Mothering Sunday, has been interpreted in various ways, and in some parts of England this day, like Mother's Day in the United States, is a time to visit mothers and grandmothers. The theme of motherhood presumably was first suggested by the reference to Jerusalem as our mother in the passage formerly appointed as the Epistle on this day (Galatians 4:21–31). (In the new Prayer Book, this charming but puzzling passage continues to be appointed for the daily office on this Sunday in alternate years.) Also, every two or three years the Feast of the Annunciation occurs during the week that precedes or follows this Sunday. This would appear to be a more useful approach to the mothering theme in years when it is applicable.

Another custom on this Sunday is the singing of hymns relating to the heavenly Jerusalem as the goal and objective of our earthly striving. Although this too was inspired by the former Epistle from Galatians, several such hymns remain very fitting for Refreshment Sunday. Peter Abelard's "O what their joy and their glory must be," Hymn 589, is especially poignant in the midst of Lent. Hymn 585, "Jerusalem, my happy home," with its reference to Our Lady in verse 4, is most felicitous in years when the relation to the Feast of the Annunciation is brought out. In such years, there will also be the opportunity to sing two great but unfamiliar Annunciation hymns, 317 and 477. As these latter two are now also proper for the Fourth Sunday of Advent, it is hoped that they may become more widely known.

For those parishes fortunate enough to have Evensong on Sunday, Mid-Lent can be a notable occasion. The singing of the "Jerusalem" hymns, the reading of the lesson from Galatians, the chanting of the *Magnificat,* the short litany "That this evening may be holy, good, and peaceful," and the new Collect for Sunday evening (Proposed Prayer Book, pages 69 and 123) will all combine to make an evening service of exceptional beauty.

15:
Planning for Holy Week

As soon as Lent begins, those who are concerned with arrangements for worship must be looking ahead to Holy Week and Easter. This is as it should be, for the whole season of Lent is intended to be, among other things, a preparation for our sacramental and spiritual participation in the dying and rising of our Blessed Lord. Clergy will necessarily meet with the leaders of choir, lay readers, altar guild, acolytes, ushers, church school, and others. The services of Holy Week and Easter Eve are so rich, so dramatic, and so filled with meaning that their potential cannot be fulfilled unless a considerable number of persons with different talents, backgrounds, and interests work together in preparation.

Parishes which do not have a regularly constituted worship committee should certainly consider having one at this time. Where there is such a committee, it may consider expanding its membership and holding additional meetings in this season. It may be helpful to open its meetings to all interested members of the congregation. Certainly a few individuals should not be left to do it all. One very effective approach at this time is to create separate "task forces" of interested persons, one to arrange for Palm Sunday, another for Maundy Thursday, another for Good Friday, and so forth. Each task force can then pursue the distinctive needs of the occasion assigned to it and can recruit the helpers it needs to decorate and arrange the church, to assemble any special equipment or utensils that are needed, to set up and reproduce a special bulletin, to secure copies of special music, and so forth.

Doing all this becomes an appropriate and interesting part of our observance of Lent. By discussing, planning, and working for Holy Week, we learn what these services mean and we also learn to look upon them as "our" services, acts of worship which express our own commitment and responsibility. Such participation in the preparation for these occasions leads naturally into the rites themselves, for on these days the liturgy has a uniquely corporate and participatory quality not matched at any other season. At other times of the Church Year, we listen to readings about certain events and we sing appropriate hymns and say appropriate prayers. At this time, we actively enter into the events being commemorated. We ourselves march with palms on Palm Sunday, we speak some of the words in the narrative of the Passion, we experience the Maundy Thursday Eucharist as a Last Supper, we mourn before the cross on Friday, we behold a pillar of fire on Saturday night. At these times, the entire congregation, in a most literal way, *does* the liturgy together.

By planning in advance and by involving the largest number of people, a worship committee will discover a wide spectrum of talents, skills, and abilities which parishioners can contribute. A small church, which may see itself as having limited resources, may in fact have a more wonderful Holy Week than the large parish in which everything is done by a professional staff. But this is not the season for competition. Every congregation, out of its own unique reality, is called to contribute its own unique gifts to the total celebration which the Church of God offers to its Creator in the observance of the holy Passover of the New Covenant.

16:
A Parade for Our King

Holy Week begins with Palm Sunday. This day is generally loved and appreciated, and a large congregation can be expected. Here is a day to express what we mean and to communicate it to a substantial number of people. Palm Sunday celebrates the kingship of Jesus Christ. How do you acclaim and honor a king? By a parade, of course. This is precisely what the Palm procession is intended to be. It is *not* simply a procession for the choir to enter the church. Nor is it simply a convenient way of distributing palms to worshipers. It is a parade for Jesus our King. Once this is understood, the liturgy of the day can be planned accordingly. Weather permitting, the procession can best start somewhere apart from the church. Large churches usually have a hall in the parish house where worshipers can gather for the opening prayer and the Palm Gospel. Small congregations may use their Sunday school area, the front porch of the rectory, or the front yard of a parishioner who lives nearby. The palms are blessed and distributed without undue delay. Each person should receive a long sliver of palm leaf, not a little folded-up cross. The purpose of this whole exercise is the parade, and the strip of palm is something to carry while marching. (Other kinds of boughs can be used also. Willow shoots were traditionally so used in England and other parts of northern Europe.)

After all have their palms, the procession can proceed out-of-doors and up the sidewalk and into the main entrance of the church. Everyone can be given a mimeographed sheet with the words of Hymn 62, "All glory, laud, and honor." In addition, Psalm 118:- 19–29 can be sung by one or more cantors, the choir and congregation singing "Hosanna in the highest" after each verse. For accompaniment during the procession, two or three brass instruments from the high-school band will do very well. For many Episcopalians such a procession will be the first time in their lives that they have marched out-of-doors for their Church. This procession is an act of worship offered to Christ, an act of witness offered to our community, and an act of devotion strengthening our own faith.

Where churches are close together, a joint procession may be undertaken. In Topeka, Kansas, during the past several years the members of St. David's Church have taken a leading role in an ecumenical Palm procession. Members of several congregations assemble for an out-of-doors blessing and the distribution of palms. They then proceed up one of the principal streets of the city, several hundred strong, with the choirs, musicians, clergy, and crucifers of the different denominations. At designated streets, the different congregations branch off to their own churches. Could not something like this be done in many other cities and towns?

Convenient directions for the palm ceremony are given in the Proposed Book of Common Prayer, pages 270–272. Previous editions of the Prayer Book suffered from the lack of any provisions whatsoever for the blessing and distribution of the palms or for the procession. It is to be noted that a bishop or priest, assisted if possible by a deacon (or additional deacons), should preside at this rite. If necessary, a deacon may preside, and if no ordained ministers are available, lay readers may lead the rite. The same is true of the special Ministry of the Word which follows, Proposed Prayer Book, pages 272–273, which we discuss in the next section. Thus all Episcopal churches, large or small, whether they have the Eucharist this day or not, and whether they have a clergyman or not, can still share in these unique and dramatic ceremonies with which Holy Week begins.

In view of what has been said above regarding the necessity of the long boughs to carry in procession, let it not be supposed that the present writer is opposed to the practice of folding strips of palm into crosses. This is something people can enjoy doing at home, with their own palms, after Sunday dinner. Some families of European background fold palms into various unusual and interesting designs. Folded or unfolded, palms (or willow boughs) may be subsequently used to decorate religious pictures or crosses in the home. Palm crosses may also be given to sick people visited during Holy Week. Those who are confined to hospital rooms will appreciate receiving them from clergy or lay visitors.

17:
The Reading of the Passion

Two days in Holy Week, Palm Sunday and Good Friday, have as a major element in their liturgy a special sort of Gospel reading known as "The Passion." In English, the word passion usually means intense excitement, love, or hate. In Latin the word means suffering, and, since many of our prayers were translated from Latin, it is frequently used in the liturgy to refer to our Lord's suffering and death. Thus, a familiar Collect originally composed by St. Thomas Aquinas speaks of the Holy Eucharist as "a memorial of his passion" (Proposed Book of Common Prayer, pages 201, 252). This word was favored by Early Christian writers because in Latin, as in English, it sounds somewhat like the word for Passover: Christian devotion emphasizes the relation between the Hebrew Passover and our celebration of the death and resurrection of our Lord.

Accordingly, the long passage in each of the four Gospels which tells of our Lord's arrest and trial, the flogging and insults by the soldiers, and his crucifixion and death, is known as the Passion. In the new lectionary, versions of St. Matthew, St. Mark, and St. Luke are read in successive years on Palm Sunday. Following a tradition of many centuries, St. John's Passion is always read on Good Friday. Because Palm Sunday is the only Sunday in the year when the account of our Savior's death is read, centuries ago it became known as the Sunday of the Passion, or simply as Passion Sunday. An alternative custom was to call the previous Sunday Passion Sunday. The latter usage was adopted into our American Prayer Book in 1928, but it has not been retained in subsequent revision as Palm Sunday has a stronger claim for this title.

Liturgically, the Passion reading is a challenge, on both Palm Sunday and Good Friday. On the one hand, the importance and spiritual significance of what is read must be clearly stressed. On the other hand, the length of the text strains both the ability of the reader and the attention of the listener. Accordingly, in the Middle Ages the custom developed of chanting the Passion dramatically, with three deacons dividing among them the parts for the narrator, Jesus, Pilate, Herod, etc. The choir spoke for the crowd. (Directions for all this can be found in the American Missal and elsewhere.) The traditional music for the Passion is hauntingly beautiful.* Congregations accustomed to plainsong will find this a musical high point of the year. Few parishes are fortunate enough to have three deacons, but custom allows priests or lay cantors to serve as "deacons of the Passion" in Holy Week. The dividing of the Passion between different readers, including lay persons, is authorized for the Episcopal Church by the rubrics of the revised liturgy (pages 273, 277).

During the Renaissance, more elaborate music was introduced into the rendering of the Passion, and finally the great passion chorales of Johann Sebastian Bach emerged. Although performed today as sacred concerts, these were originally intended as acts of worship in the Lutheran observance of Holy Week.

Instead of chanting the Passion in the traditional manner, many congregations now have it spoken by different readers, with the whole congregation serving as the crowd. If desired, it is possible to include a great many people in special roles: one group of men can be the soldiers, another group the chief priests, a woman can be Pilate's wife, someone else can read the quotations from the Old Testament, and so forth. Many options are possible as to the number of persons to be included. Each year the arrangement for Palm Sunday will differ somewhat because of differences in the details of

---

*The music is available from *Music for Liturgy,* 815 Second Avenue, New York, N.Y. 10017.

the narrative. In any case, this is a powerful liturgical experience, and you will not fail to be gripped when you hear the words "Crucify him!" emerging from your own throat.

One possibility is to have the Passion said by a group of readers on the Sunday, and then have it sung in the traditional manner on Good Friday. Most parishes can only get part of their choir to serve at any given time on Good Friday, and hence their musical capability is limited. Since the chanting of the Passion, however, depends almost entirely on the three solo chanters, the rest of the choir is not necessary. Persons who have heard the Passion read on Sunday and are familiar with its general contents, will no doubt be better equipped to appreciate the plainsong rendering on Friday. It will by no means be simple repetition, however, as St. John's Passion differs from the others at a number of points.

If the Passion is to be read dramatically, may it not also be enhanced by costumes, spears, helmets, and stage setting? Liturgical tradition answers, No. It is true that in parts of Germany and elsewhere, the passion play has developed as a lofty form of Christian theater. Such plays are not an actual part of the liturgy, however, and they demand very high standards in order to be acceptable. The liturgical Passion is so solemn, and it expresses such grief, that a theatrical rendering of it is out of place. Carefully read words can, in this case, be as emotionally charged as is suitable to the context. Where desired, however, it is possible to plan and rehearse at suitable points the entry and movement of the different readers in the chancel. Certain restrained gestures may also be appropriate. The present writer has served in a congregation where a young woman planned all of this, reproduced and marked the text for each reader, and supervised two brief rehearsals, after which the Passion was splendidly rendered on Palm Sunday morning with a deeply impressed congregation.

On Palm Sunday, after the procession and Passion, most priests will be willing to confine their sermon to a few well chosen sentences, and most organists will be content with a few short hymns. (The hymns which follow should be about our Lord's Passion, not about the triumphal entry which was celebrated in the procession.) The permission of the new Prayer Book to omit the Nicene Creed and the General Confession on this occasion (page 273) is welcome. This is not simply a matter of saving time, but rather a matter of focus and emphasis. Palm Sunday, of all the Sundays in the year, has its own distinct and unique liturgical features. These should not be obscured by immediately overlaying them with every other thing that we do on every other Sunday. This solemn Sunday of the Passion is not supposed to be theatrical, but it certainly should be dramatic in the best sense of that noble word. True dramatic art is characterized by good taste, good judgment, and a clear sense of priorities.

18:
The Eve of the Crucifixion

Most congregations now have their principal Maundy Thursday service in the evening. In some parishes, it has been the custom to interrupt the normal Lenten routine and get out white vestments for the Eucharist, to sing the *Gloria in excelsis,* and to treat the occasion as the "Birthday of the Blessed Sacrament." Such an approach raises some questions. The Last Supper was just that —the final meal of a man about to suffer execution. No doubt this final meal had its element of joy, but this is hardly the time to forget about Lent. Scholarship has reminded us, furthermore, that the Jewish day begins at sundown. Maundy Thursday evening is thus the beginning of Good Friday. People sometimes ask why Holy Communion is not commonly administered in the Episcopal Church on Good Friday. The ultimate answer, in the opinion of some of us, is that the Maundy Thursday evening Eucharist *is* the Good Friday Communion. This may affect our view of how Maundy Thursday should be celebrated.

Some parishes seek to replicate the Last Supper by having the Eucharist in conjunction with an actual parish supper. Some re-enact a Jewish Passover meal, or *seder.* The latter can certainly have great impact and meaning. In many parishes, however, experience has shown it to be more effective to have a *seder* early in Lent, as a basis for discussion and learning. In this way, any confusion of thought between the Jewish and Christian meanings of the bread and wine can be avoided. In any case, when the Eucharist is actually celebrated at a table with other food, it would seem common courtesy, both to our Lord and to the communicants, to differentiate very clearly between the bread and wine that are consecrated and those that are not. In a sense, Jesus hallowed all bread, and he is concerned with all the hungry people of the world, and we must never forget this. At the same time, what is consecrated is different, and has a unique meaning which, on Maundy Thursday (of all times), should not be obscured. It is regrettable that further confusion has sometimes been created by the use of unauthorized forms of consecration. In view of the several eucharistic prayers now legally approved for use in the Episcopal Church, it would seem that ample latitude is provided.

The most neglected aspect of the Maundy Thursday liturgy is precisely one of its oldest and most distinctive features: the washing of feet. The provisions for this day in the Proposed Prayer Book call attention to this ancient tradition. In the course of Christian history, footwashing has been carried out in various ways and in various circumstances. Among the many possible ways of doing it, we would commend a simple and practical procedure which can be carried out in a reverent manner in an ordinary parish which desires this ceremony.

First, a dozen or so persons must be invited to have their feet washed. It is suggested that a variety of ages and types in the parish be chosen. The procedure should be clearly explained to them beforehand so that they may wear shoes and socks that can be easily removed. In the church, seats should be placed beforehand in a convenient and conspicuous position. It is suggested that a row of six chairs be placed on each side of the sanctuary facing the altar (sideways to the congregation). A bowl (such as the large aluminum bowls which can be readily bought at a hardware store) should be placed to the right and the left of the altar, each with a large pitcher filled with lukewarm water, and a towel. If desired, a long piece of terry cloth can be used, so that it can be wrapped around the minister's waist, as in St. John 13:4.

The Eucharist begins in the usual manner and proceeds through the Gospel. A brief homily can follow, simply stating that we will now do what our Lord has directed. It all requires very little explanation and no moralizing. The twelve persons should then come forward, take their seats, and at once remove their shoes and socks. The priest removes his chasuble if he has been wearing one, and takes the towel at one end of the altar. He kneels in front of the first person, as does a server. The priest holds the person's feet over the bowl and briefly washes them, while the server pours water from the pitcher. The priest then dries them with the towel, and moves on his knees to the next person, for whom the same procedure is repeated. All this requires only a few seconds per person, and six persons' feet are easily washed within two minutes. Meanwhile, at the other side of the sanctuary, an assistant priest, another minister, lay reader, vestryman, or other suitable person, accompanied by another server, may wash the feet of the other row of persons. If there are more clergy or more servers to be included, each "washer" can have two assistants. In any case, it may be a great advantage to have two rows of persons having their feet washed simultaneously; thus, no individual is embarrassed by having the entire attention focused on him or her at any given moment. All of this is very easily carried out. Meanwhile, the congregation can sing or say suitable verses, as in the Maundy Thursday Proper, Proposed Prayer Book, pages 274–275. Perhaps, however, it is better to leave the singing to the choir at this time so that the congregation can simply watch.

The service continues with the Prayers of the People. It is recommended that one of the shorter sets, such as Form III (page 387), Form IV (page 388), or Form VI (page 392), be used at this time. Meanwhile, those whose feet were washed will have gotten their shoes and socks back on. At the Peace they can be greeted by the other persons in the sanctuary and then return to their pews and greet those around them. Thus a sense of identification with the washing of feet may be suggested to everyone. For the Great Thanksgiving, Eucharistic Prayer D (pages 372–375), with its rather full reference to the Last Supper, is especially appropriate. Because it has a place for some intercessions within it, a short form for the Prayers of the People was recommended earlier.

After the service, it is customary for the ministers and servers (assisted by others, if desired) to remove all the candlesticks, altar cloths, etc., from the sanctuary, so that the holy table will be bare on Good Friday and ready for cleaning and fresh linens on Saturday in preparation for Easter. Psalm 22 is appropriately recited during the stripping of the altar. The congregation may remain kneeling for this.

V

The Easter Season

19:
Easter as a Season

Before settling on plans for the liturgy on Easter Day, we need to give some thought to the fact that this feast is not just one day but an entire season of fifty days. Nothing less does justice to what Easter signifies, and a renewed emphasis on this season has been one of the major objectives of the liturgical movement of the twentieth century.

The Great Fifty Days are traditionally the most joyous part of the Christian Year. They begin with Easter Day and conclude with Whitsunday or Pentecost. (The word Pentecost is Greek for fiftieth.) This is the oldest section of the Christian Year; the other seasons grew up around it. Lent originated quite specifically as a preparation for this Easter season. It is a strange irony that many church people try faithfully during Lent to observe forty days of preparation, yet virtually abandon Eastertide after going to church on Easter Day.

At the spiritual level, we must all seek to sustain the spirit of the Resurrection through these seven weeks. At the practical level, we must seek ways to express and communicate this spirit. Equally important, we must try to identify and eliminate items which implicitly undermine and weaken the spirit of this season. The new Prayer Book offers us many positive resources for celebrating this season, in the Holy Eucharist, in the daily offices, and, to some extent, in other special rites and sacraments. It remains for all of us in our local congregations to utilize these resources to best advantage. We also need to examine critically customs and habits which impede the full celebration of the Great Fifty Days. Let us consider some specifics.

First there is the area of preaching and teaching. The kind of sermon on Easter Day which attempts to cover the entire topic of the Resurrection, leaving the following weeks for entirely different and unrelated topics, is not helpful. Sermons at the Easter Vigil and on Easter morning should be part of a larger plan, extending through the whole season. This does not mean that the preacher must plan his sermons several weeks in advance, but it does mean he should look over the entire Great Fifty Days and be sensitive to the period as a whole. The same is true for those teaching. They certainly have plenty of subject matter. The whole period celebrates the victory of Christ and the communication of that victory to his followers. The Christian Easter takes up and includes the meaning of the Old Testament Passover. The Passover celebrates God's creative and regenerative power manifested in nature in the spring, and also his power in history manifested in the deliverance of the Hebrews from slavery in Egypt. Christ's royal high priesthood and heavenly intercession deserve more attention than they usually receive. The communion of saints is also a theme of this season. Finally, one is not simply left with one Sunday to hear about the Holy Spirit. Bible readings on the different Sundays make it clear that the gift of the Holy Spirit to the Church is being celebrated throughout the entire period.

Secondly, there is the music. Many parishes have several Easter hymns on Easter Day, some the next Sunday, and then quickly taper it off. True, it is difficult to sing "Jesus Christ is risen *today*" four or five weeks afterwards. On the other hand, some outstanding Easter hymns, such as "At the Lamb's high feast we sing" (Hymn 89) are very usable throughout the period. With planning, such hymns can be distributed through these Sundays, using the best ones twice at two- or three-week intervals. In addition, a number of hymns classed in the Hymnal as "general hymns" are in fact especially appropriate to this time of year. "Alleluia! Sing to Jesus!" (347) and "Ye watchers and ye holy ones" (599) are obvious winners, being among our most popular and most characteristically Anglican hymns. Hymns 207, 279, 345, 357, 583, and 587 are among other good hymns suitable for these weeks.

Then there is the appearance of the church. Just as there is a tendency at Christmas to bank the sanctuary with poinsettias, so one often sees sanctuaries overwhelmed with lilies on Easter Day. In both cases, everyone knows that this impressive exhibition is essentially for one day. It subtly expresses a theatrical view of worship very congenial to those well-meaning and casual worshipers who come only on these two days and for weddings and funerals. A more constructive approach is to apportion the money donated for flowers throughout the season, so that a reasonably festive appearance can be maintained for all seven weeks. In many parishes, parishioners will be able to bring flowers from their own backyards each week. Branches of lilac, dogwood, and other blooming bushes or trees make outstanding decorations, eloquently testifying to the power of God in the natural world. It is appropriate in Eastertide to put flowers not only at the altar but also around the pulpit, lectern, font, and paschal candle.

Many of our parishes have a paschal candle, but most Episcopalians have little idea what it is. Let it be conspicuously placed where the Gospel is proclaimed. Its symbolic meaning is certainly worth at least one sermon for grown-ups and at least one church school lesson for youngsters during the course of the season. An "Easter Garden" will be discussed in the next section. Banners and other special decorations may also be used throughout this season.

In every congregation, there are also a variety of small things which connote the difference between a feast and "business as usual." As we learn to see this, we can correct many unnecessary bad habits! In thinking of the Easter Season as a whole, and planning for it as a whole, we come to see Easter Day in a new perspective. It can, by the grace of God, become the beginning, rather than the end, of a period of great joy.

20:
An Easter Garden

An interesting kind of decoration to set up in church before the first service of Easter is an "Easter Garden." Such gardens have been customarily used in many Anglican parishes in England and other parts of the world for many years, but are a comparative rarity in the United States. An Easter Garden is a small, simulated garden with a door to the empty tomb. It can be an interesting and beautiful expression of devotion, giving vivid expression to our awareness of the great fact of Easter: that Jesus Christ did, indeed, rise from the dead on the first day of the week. It symbolizes also the conviction of Catholic Christians that there is an underlying unity between the Creation and the Resurrection.

An Easter Garden will usually be several square yards in extent. It can be created in a side chapel, a transept, or in the front of the church. Large congregations at Easter, however, will usually preclude anything that blocks the approaches to the altar at this time. An ideal place for an Easter Garden is often in the area immediately surrounding the font. If there is a rarely used doorway in the back or side of the church, this may, perhaps, be used for the doorway to the tomb. This can be especially effective if there is a small arched doorway in a stone church. In some places, especially in warm climates, an Easter Garden may be created out of doors. In an urban church, it may be possible to set it up in an area that is visible from the sidewalk. Usually the garden will be created of rows of flowers or other plants in pots or vases. Some of these can be purchased or cut for the purpose. In many parishes there will be parishioners who would be glad to lend house plants for this if they are assured that their plants will be carefully tended.

If the church does not have a stone floor, the watering of the plants may present some hazard to the floor surface. This problem can be solved by purchasing from the hardware store an inexpensive plastic sheet which can be spread over the area that is to be occupied by the garden. The edges of it can be secured to the floor with heavy-duty tape.

The plants can be arranged so as to leave a path to the font, if that is within the center of the garden, and to the mouth of the tomb. Borders to the path can be emphasized by laying down rows of bricks—without mortar, of course. A low wall of dry bricks may also be laid along one or two sides of the garden. Mellow old bricks can usually be secured from dealers in secondhand building supplies. They are not expensive. For borders and edges of an Easter Garden about ten feet square, we would suggest that about 100 bricks would be needed. If a low wall is to be built, you will probably need 200. (Bricks can also serve other purposes if you have various decorations or things to be mounted during the year. They can, for instance, be useful in setting up a large crèche at Christmas.)

If a real doorway is used as the door for the tomb, the space within it can be filled with a banner saying "He is risen" or something of the sort. If, on the other hand, the doorway into the tomb has to be totally created, a small arched opening can be cut in a large piece of cardboard painted grey. Or a simple wooden frame can be tied or nailed together and several yards of crumpled aluminum foil can be shaped over it in the form of a stone cliff with a cavelike opening. The foil can be sprayed with grey or tan paint so as to resemble stone. In the doorway, a picture of an angel can be mounted, or a banner used, or other appropriate visual material. A more ambitious approach is to leave enough space inside the doorway so as to present the linen cloths lying on the floor (see John 20:6–7).

Local circumstances and ingenuity will suggest many possibilities for beautifying an Easter Garden.

The plan, however must be completed and all the materials, tools and utensils stored in or near the church during Holy Week. Thus, everything can be quickly arranged and installed in the limited time between the last service of Good Friday and the first service of Easter.

If baptisms are performed at Eastertime, as we hope will be the case, an Easter Garden provides a very striking setting for the font, and gives visual expression to the theological relationship between the sacrament of Holy Baptism and our Lord's rising from the grave. During the Easter Vigil, or any other time when baptism is administered, candles can be placed among the flowers. If baptism is done by immersion (which is very easy with small children) a large enough tub for this purpose can be set up and flowers and branches can be placed around it so that it does not look unsightly. The author has often used a large galvanized tub painted with simple evangelical colors: blue, gold, red, green, all of which harmonize well with the flowers, ribbons, colored candles, vestments, ladies' evening dresses, etc., of the Great Vigil of the Resurrection.

In some ethnic traditions, there are other ways of arranging an Easter Garden. Among the Polish, for instance, men in soldiers' uniforms guard the tomb from Good Friday until Easter morning, when a messenger chases them away, crying, "He is risen." The Eastern Orthodox have a sepulchre in which an icon of the dead Christ, painted on cloth, is "buried" on Good Friday. Various other customs worth investigating also exist.

How long should an Easter Garden be kept in place? In some parishes it is dismantled almost at once and the potted flowers are all given to children in the congregation. Where such a distribution is desired, small plants for the children can in fact be included with larger ones to be kept in the church for a longer period. A well-arranged Easter Garden certainly deserves to be kept in place through the following Sunday. Or it may be kept through Rogation Sunday, when it relates to the themes of the day. In fact the author has encountered no difficulty in keeping such a garden, populated with common varieties of house plants, in good color until Whitsunday.

21:
The Great Vigil of Easter

During recent years, growing numbers of persons in different Churches have been finding that the most adequate service of worship for "the Queen of Feasts" is the Easter Vigil. This is a service for Saturday night which gathers together striking ceremonies, readings of Holy Scripture, and the administration of "the two Great Sacraments" on a most dramatic, impressive, and solemn scale.

Perhaps ideally, the vigil takes place at midnight, or it may begin before sunrise. Many parishes would prefer to have it soon after the Saturday sunset, however, so that families with children of all ages can attend. It begins with the kindling of a fire. This may be in a container at the back of the church, or it may be a real bonfire out-of-doors. From this fire, the large paschal candle is lit and carried in procession into the dark church. This great candle is then consecrated by a long and remarkable prayer sequence known as the *Exsultet*, "Rejoice now, heavenly hosts and choirs of angels." This is traditionally sung by a deacon. If no deacon is available, or if he cannot sing, a priest or lay cantor may do it. It is one of the most beautiful things in all Christian liturgy.

The vigil office then follows. It includes a succession of great passages from the Old Testament, normally beginning with the story of Creation (Genesis 1:1–2:2) and including the story of the Exodus (Exodus 14:10–15:1). Each lesson is followed by a chant or hymn, and a prayer. The present writer prefers to include the sermon in this part of the service, but it may come later.

The third section of the vigil is devoted to Christian Initiation. If candidates, young or adult, are available, Holy Baptism should by all means be administered, for it is in a unique sense the sacrament of the Resurrection. Where the bishop is available, confirmation can also be given. In any case, however, the entire congregation can renew its baptismal vows.

The fourth section of the vigil is the Holy Eucharist, in which we meet the risen Lord in the Breaking of Bread. For this, of course, the finest vestments and vessels of the parish are used, and the sanctuary is decorated in the most festive manner. After the service, worshipers will remain for a party with suitable food and drink, and perhaps more singing.

Such a service has to be seen to be believed. The awareness of the awakening of creation in the spring, the recalling of the Jewish Passover, the celebration of the reality of Jesus' Resurrection and his gift of the Holy Spirit to his people—all of this is a dynamic combination of spiritual forces united in one great liturgical drama. "It is a night much to be remembered"(Exodus 12:42).

The text of the service (Proposed Prayer Book, pages 284–295) should be carefully studied.* Its complexity is such that it is not easily undertaken by people who have never seen it before. If your parish wishes to adopt it and no one is familiar with the rite, a first step is for as many people as possible to go *this* year to a nearby parish which has it. Then you can organize it in your own parish *next* year. Another approach is for a group of parishes to band together to hold the vigil in a central location. For several years, at Roanridge we have had a vigil to which we invited clergy and laity from nearby parts of Missouri and Kansas. We urged visiting clergy to vest, and likewise encouraged acolytes, readers, and others from different parishes to take active parts. As a result, a growing number of local parishes learned to arrange their own vigils. The first year the vigil is introduced, only twenty or thirty people may come. After two or three years it draws a crowd. Rectors find that this does not

---

*For a helpful discussion see *The Great Vigil of Easter: A Commentary,* Associated Parishes, Inc., 1977.

hurt attendance at Easter morning services. Many of those who come Saturday night are so excited that they return again Sunday morning.

One of the great things about the vigil is that a responsible part may be played by any individual, family, or group in the parish. Before the service, a number of people will need to work to prepare the church and the place where the party is held after the vigil. Many kinds of decorations may be arranged. Boughs of forsythia, fresh dogwood, or other spring flowers may be contributed by members of the congregation. Some parishes buy a plain white paschal candle and a talented parishioner designs and paints decorations on it. Some years ago I saw a large and beautiful paschal candle which a youth group had made. (They boiled down candle stubs saved throughout the previous year.)

In the service itself, any number of acolytes, choristers, and ushers can be used. Several lay readers are needed for the Old Testament Lessons and the Epistle. As to the clergy, appropriate functions can be shared by as many deacons and priests as are available, and of course a visiting bishop or two will also be most welcome. On the other hand, one clergyman with several knowledgeable lay assistants can manage quite well. For music, besides the customary organ accompaniment, other available instruments can be used to great advantage. At one vigil the author has participated in, a high point occurred after the Exodus reading, when a black soloist sang "Go down, Moses." For the party after the service, people gladly contribute cold cuts, colored eggs, cheese, cakes, bottles of wine, soft drinks, and so forth. On such a night we learn to exchange with conviction the ancient Christian Easter greeting:

Christ is risen.
He is risen indeed.

22:
Thomas Sunday

The Sunday following Easter Day presents a liturgical challenge. Inevitably there is a sense of descent from the heights of the Sunday of the Resurrection. Yet, if we believe that Easter is to be observed not just on one Sunday but during a season spanning several Sundays, then this must be affirmed clearly and strongly at once—not a month later.

The new lectionary obligingly assists us in making this a more important day by extending the Gospel reading to the entire second half of the twentieth chapter of St. John. Thus it includes all that was previously read, but it goes on to include the appearance of the risen Christ to St. Thomas. The new lectionary provides other suitable choices each year for the earlier readings, but this Gospel is always the same.

It is an extremely valuable passage. Let us examine it. Late Easter afternoon, Jesus appears to his disciples, shows himself alive, and blesses them with his peace (St. John 20: 19–20). Then he commissions them as apostles ("persons who are sent"), breathes on them the Holy Spirit, and gives them power to forgive sins (verses 21–23). Reflecting on this, we will see the parallelism between the gifts of the risen Christ and what we affirm in the third paragraphs of the Apostles' and Nicene Creeds. Then, "eight days later" (verse 26) the scene is repeated. Eight days, in the idiom of that age, means what we call seven days. (They counted the first and last days of a span of time: thus Friday to Sunday were "three days.") In other words, it is the first day of the next week, the following Sunday—the day we are talking about. Our Lord manifests himself to doubting Thomas, and says, "Blessed are those who have not seen and yet believe" (verses 26–29). Thomas was, of course, where we are. We do not find it easy to believe. Some of us, sad to say, may even have missed church on Easter. We must take the word of others for the truth of the Resurrection. Yet the Lord will bless our faith, halting though it be. This episode restores to the Sunday after the Resurrection a distinctive commemoration of its own, a particular event on this very day. It also has a wider bearing. Here, St. John suggests, the followers of Jesus are learning where and when to meet him: in the assembly of his followers on the first day of the week, the day they soon came to call the Lord's Day. This is what all the Sundays of Eastertide are about, and they in turn provide the pattern for all other Sundays of the year. On the Lord's Day we assemble in God's name, united to the risen Christ and to one another, by the power of the Holy Spirit.

The restoration of "Thomas Sunday" fills in a useful part of the total Easter narrative. Hitherto, we have only had this episode in the liturgical Gospel on the Feast of St. Thomas shortly before Christmas (21 December), when the passage seemed to many people strangely out of context and in any case received little attention. Getting this event back into its original setting also has a further advantage in terms of hymnody. Hymn 98, "That Easter Day with joy was bright," is highly appropriate, and the great Hymn 99, "O sons and daughters," has verses specially for this occasion. For the best effect, Hymn 99 should not be sung until after the Gospel; it may well serve as an offertory or final hymn. For other hymns, several of the familiar Easter ones are quite suitable. Depending on the sermon topic, a hymn relating to saints (such as 600) or apostles (such as 599) or heaven (such as 587) may be chosen.

23:
Fulfilling the Great Fifty Days

A quarter of a century and more ago, I was fortunate in often being able to visit the Mission Farm at Sherburne Center in the Green Mountains of Vermont. There Father Truman Heminway and his wife Gertrude supported themselves mainly by farming, provided a place for retreats and spiritual counsel, and ministered to many people from many parts of America by providing a new vision of the Church and the Christian way of life. I can well remember Father Truman, stroking his grey beard, and pronouncing in his powerful deep voice that the trouble with the Episcopal Church was that it had not revived the Great Fifty Days.

I had just learned in seminary what the Great Fifty Days were (the fifty-day period from Easter through Whitsunday), so I agreed dutifully, although I had no idea how one was supposed to "revive" them. It seemed to me then that the Episcopal Church had many greater problems. (Back in those days, the big issue was whether or not there should be a special bishop to serve the Armed Forces.) After twenty-five years, I am not so sure that there are "many greater problems."

The Great Fifty Days celebrate the proclamation of the Resurrection, the hope of life eternal, the knowledge that Christ has triumphed over sin and suffering and death, the faith that the ascended Lord is our high priest ever interceding for us, and the awareness of the living presence of his Holy Spirit in the Church. All of this is precisely the good news of the Gospel. This is the "paschal mystery" which is the heart of Christianity. To communicate this mystery, to enable people to experience the reality of it, to help the lives of individuals and communities be transformed by it—all of this is indeed central to the purpose of the Christian

Church. If we are not addressing ourselves to this, then this is indeed "the trouble with the Episcopal Church."

Meanwhile, it is truly remarkable that in so short a time, what was an odd question a generation ago is at least being taken seriously by many members of the Church. Now we are engaged in adopting a new Prayer Book in which emphasis on the fifty days of the Easter season is a striking characteristic of the book as a whole. Let us glance at some of the ways in which this emphasis is expressed in the principal service.

In the Holy Eucharist, the Easter opening Acclamation with its Alleluias establishes the theme of the season at the very beginning. The *Gloria in excelsis* soon follows. The heart of the first half of the liturgy is the Bible reading and the preaching normally based on it. For the Ministry of the Word of God, our new three-year cycle of readings provides a distinctive pattern for the six Sundays and the Feast of the Ascension which come in between Easter Day and Pentecost.

For the three readings at the liturgy, the first is either from the Acts of the Apostles, or from the Old Testament. The use of Acts during this season follows an ancient tradition alluded to by St. Augustine of Hippo, among others. It is a unique feature of these Sundays, reminding us that the coming of the Holy Ghost to the Apostolic Church is being celebrated throughout this entire season. The appropriateness of Acts is increased by the fact that most of these passages contain sermons in which the Apostles proclaim the Resurrection.

The three-year cycle, as originally planned, did not include Old Testament readings in Eastertide, but because of the close relation between the Hebrew Passover and Easter, it was soon recognized that some preachers would desire Old Testament texts, at least in some years. Hence an Old Testament passage, instead of Acts, may be used for the first reading. Many of the favorite psalms are appointed and are particularly appropriate after the first reading.

For the second reading, the passage from Acts may be used if it was not used as the first reading, or there may be an Epistle. These are usually from the First Epistle of St. John or the First Epistle of

St. Peter—both have long been recognized as specially suitable for this season. In Year C, we have some beautiful passages from Revelation which we have not heard before at the Eucharist, affirming the resurrection of the dead, the communion of saints, and the life of the world to come. The use of Revelation in Eastertide was, many centuries ago, the custom of the ancient Gallican Liturgy of Western Europe.

The Holy Gospel is almost always from St. John, and on different weeks contains some of the best-loved passages—"I am the good shepherd," "because I live you will live also," "a new commandment I give you," "that they may all be one . . ." These passages were selected not only for their beauty but because they express so well the continuing relationship between the risen Christ and his followers, and at the same time speak repeatedly of the promise of the Holy Spirit.

Moving to the second half of the liturgy, where Rite I is used, the themes of the season are clearly articulated in the Proper Prefaces to be used. Eucharistic Prayer II would seem especially fitting for this season. Following the Breaking of the Bread, an appropriate variation at this time is to use, in place of the usual *Agnus Dei* and Prayer of Humble Access, a suitable hymn, such as 89, 206, 207, or 357.

Rite II offers us four different eucharistic prayers. We cannot say that any one of them should not be used at this season, or that one should be used to the exclusion of the others. The Easter season is so rich in meaning that it touches on each of them in some particular way. Prayers A and B have the Proper Prefaces, and the entire Preface is easily singable. The concluding doxology of both of these prayers is identical and also singable. Prayer C has its unique way of celebrating both the Creation and the Resurrection. Prayer D expresses all the themes of the season with fullness, including the communion of saints at the end.*

---

*For an analysis of these four eucharistic prayers and their origins, see *The Holy Eucharist, Rite Two: A Commentary*, Associated Parishes, Inc., 1976, pp. 10–13.

Finally, both Rite I and Rite II have Alleluias to add to the concluding Dismissal. So at the end we go on our several ways, bound to the risen Christ and one another by the power of his promised Holy Spirit.

24:
Rogation Sunday

A major aspect of the paschal mystery is the unveiling of the transcendent power of God in creation. The Great Vigil of Easter begins, as does the Bible itself and the Creed, by affirming God as Creator. When Christians see spring flowers, hear the songs of birds, relish the first radishes and scallions from the garden ("bitter herbs"), we do so with a perception far beyond the sentimental pleasure of the secular world. We are enjoying the harbingers of a renewed creation, the signs of the God who is himself, as St. Augustine says,

Ever old, ever new, yet making all things new.

The doctrine of Creation has great urgency today with the crisis of world food production, the exhaustion of natural resources, and the widespread reluctance to enforce strict environmental controls. All these issues involve difficult questions deserving the most serious thought and prayer. The Christian conviction as to the goodness of the natural world and its place in the providence of God are major considerations which are important for the Church to affirm.

The place of Creation within the mystery of Easter is most dramatically expressed in the Great Vigil, with the hallowing of the paschal candle, the reading of the account of Creation with the Spirit hovering over the waters and the creation of light, followed a little while later (if there is a baptism) by the invoking of the Holy Spirit over the water of the font.

The theme of Creation comes to the fore again in the latter part of the Easter Season with the so-called Rogation Days. These are the Monday, Tuesday, and Wednesday preceding the Feast of our

Lord's Ascension, and they are the traditional times to ask God's blessing on crops, herds, and other sources of food. In some places this is extended to include forests, mines, factories, and other places of human work and employment. Historic editions of the Book of Common Prayer treated these as penitential times, listing the Rogation Days among the days of fasting and abstinence. This penitential intrusion into the Easter season has not seemed appropriate and the listing of these days in reference to fasting and abstinence was removed from the American Prayer Book in 1928. The present Proposed Book does not suggest any interruption of the spirit of the Easter season at this point, but the daily office continues to have traditional Rogationtide readings on these days. Suitable prayers for agriculture, for towns and rural areas, for natural resources, and related topics will be found in the Prayers and Thanksgivings section. There are also Rogation Masses provided, which may be used either on these days or at other times when prayers are to be offered for crops, for rain, and so forth. They are adaptable to a number of occasions.

For most churchgoers, it is of course on the preceding Sunday that the celebration of the Rogation themes will be experienced. On this Sixth Sunday of Easter, as on other Sundays of the season, the first of the appointed scriptural readings may either be a passage from the Book of Acts, or an Old Testament Lesson. In Year B, the selection from Acts speaks of the sharing of food in time of famine; the other two years offer St. Paul's great sermons at Athens and Lystra, respectively, affirming God's witness to himself in the Creation. The Old Testament readings in all three years express Rogationtide themes, as do the psalms. The second reading for the liturgy comes from one of the non-Pauline Epistles or Revelation, or the passage from Acts may be used if it was not used before. The Gospel is always from St. John, as in the preceding and following weeks. Year A gives the Parable of the Vine, which is concluded in Year B. In Year C, the passage from Revelation speaks of the river of the water of life, nourishing the tree of life with its ever-bearing fruit and its leaves for the healing of the nations. All of this provides ample opportunity to celebrate Creation and the transformation of Creation in Christ. Here too can be expressed the distinctly paschal theme of God's manifestation of himself within his Creation to those whose eyes are brightened by the perception of the blessed hope he has put before us.

In addition to those hymns customarily associated with Rogationtide, we would recommend hymns 92, 301, and 281. The latter should always be sung to the great Beethoven tune (from the Ninth Symphony) for which the author intended it, and with which it will be found in the hymnals of many other denominations, and in *The Hymnal Supplement Number Two*.

Rogationtide offers exceptional opportunities for interesting and creative decorations in the church. Depending on the climate and the part of the country, stalks of grain or other locally available foodstuffs may be available. In many localities parishioners can contribute locally grown flowers and boughs of blooming trees and shrubs. Food in different stages of processing, or other products, may also be exhibited and perhaps referred to in the sermon.

Meanwhile, the secular world has long since adopted our Rogation Days for what is variously called Soil Stewardship Week or Natural Resources Week. The principal organization encouraging this observance is the National Association of Conservation Districts (NACD) which publishes a variety of printed materials each year available at a nominal price for churches, schools, clubs, etc. An attractive booklet published annually discusses soil conservation questions and agricultural issues as viewed in a broadly Christian context. The use of such material from a "secular" source may serve to remind us all that the message of the Church sometimes reaches far beyond her own borders. These resources can be ordered from NACD Service Dept., P.O. Box 855, League City, Texas 77573., or obtained from local Conservation Districts anywhere in the United States.

25:
The Feast of the Ascension

The Holy Thursday of our Lord's Ascension into heaven usually does not receive the attention it deserves. In some parishes I have visited, the rector does not even mention it in the announcements on the preceding Sunday. The fact that it is the only major feast of the year which invariably comes in the middle of the week no doubt has affected its observance. Yet one also hears it said that Sunday church attendance declines in the spring because many people go away on weekends. If this is true, then there is also something positive in the fact that this feast occurs in midweek.

Of course Thursday is a customary day for a midweek Eucharist in many congregations (often at 10:00 AM) and a small but faithful congregation can be counted on. This does not do justice to the great feast, however. Nor does it really help to have the clergy endlessly complain that the laity do not come to church enough. A full-fledged celebration of Our Lord's Ascension requires thought and planning. Looked at nontheologically, Ascension Day has three potential assets. First, as said, it is unique in that it is always in the middle of the week. Secondly, it has some of the best hymns in the Hymnal. Thirdly, it comes at a time when beautiful weather prevails all over the United States. In terms of planning, these three characteristics add up to *an evening service with a strong musical program.*

Well in advance, it can be made clear to the choir that this is one of those several special feasts each year when attendance is highly important. Many choirs practice on Thursday night anyhow, and this week the service can replace the practice. They can be given a part in the service that they will find gratifying and enjoyable. Besides the usual organ accompaniment (or instead of it), on this occasion two or three other instruments can be secured. In the warm Southern States an out-of-door Eucharist may be planned on a lawn, terrace, or courtyard adjacent to the church, and brass accompaniment will be helpful. The presence of choir and musicians immediately establishes the importance of this feast in the mind of the congregation. It becomes a "real" feast. Great Ascension Day hymns in the Episcopal Hymnal include not only hymns 102, 103, and 104, but also 347, 351, 352, 355, 356, 357, and others. Several of this group were certainly written to be Ascension hymns, and among them are some of the finest and best-loved of all our hymns.

In ecclesiastical tradition, Whitsunday, rather than Ascension Day, is the preferable date for Holy Baptism at this time of year. Yet some congregations may prefer baptisms on Ascension. To administer this sacrament having heard the Ascension Day reading from Acts certainly provides a striking sequence. One church in the diocese may also be fortunate enough to secure the bishop on this evening and have confirmation as well as baptism. The new combined rite of Baptism, Confirmation, and Eucharist, together with sermon and hymns, can be carried out in an hour.

One option is to have the service at seven o'clock, and have a potluck supper at eight. Episcopalians used to joke about parish suppers, but in the experience of this writer, potluck meals are usually delicious. On this occasion many congregations will find it appropriate to have wine served. After the meal, the musicians could lead some singing for a few minutes, or play for half an hour of dancing. Another option is to show a good contemporary film of religious significance after the supper. No matter how the supper is concluded, however, the kind of Ascension observance we are proposing will be a significant and memorable observance of a major item in the history of our salvation.

We have not mentioned the paschal candle. In some places the extinguishing of it during the reading of the Ascension Gospel has been emphasized. In some larger parishes, it is ceremonially extinguished at two or three different services on Ascension Day, and again at every service on the following Sunday! To many church-men, this seems like a ceremonial rejection of what the candle symbolizes. At the Ascension, our Lord withdrew his visible pres-ence from a particular time and place in Palestine, so that he could be invisibly present with his followers everywhere and at all times. Hence, the new Prayer Book follows the ancient custom of keeping the paschal candle burning through Whitsunday. It is not cermoni-ally extinguished on that day, but instead it may be moved to a position near the font where it may be appropriately relighted whenever baptism is administered, and perhaps on certain other occasions as well. During the past twenty years, this custom of using the paschal candle at baptism has become widespread in both Europe and America.

26:
Pentecost or Whitsunday

Pentecost is the Greek word for fiftieth. This feast is the fiftieth and final day of the Easter or Paschal season. As the Holy Spirit brought to the apostles the power to proclaim everywhere the Resurrection of our Lord, so this day brings to the season of the Resurrection a final and concluding climax. Eastertide does not taper off or wither away: it ends gloriously with the projection of the Easter message into every land and into every subsequent period of history.

Obviously this day should be emphasized, planned for, and observed as one of the major days of the Christian Year. Some parishes quite properly make an effort to encourage every active communicant to receive the Holy Sacrament on this day. If a public baptism can be arranged or the bishop can administer confirmation in your parish at this time, that is a fortunate bonus. In this case, one may take advantage of the rubric (Proposed Prayer Book, page 888) and lengthen the reading from the Book of Acts to include the account of the original baptisms on Pentecost. The entire second chapter of Acts may be read, and this may well be preferred in churches that have a Pentecost Vigil with the ample time it allows. For a Sunday morning service when time is limited, we would recommend Acts 2:1–11,14,23–26,37–42.

On the lighter side, in some congregations everyone is asked to wear something red. Can't you get a trumpeter or trombonist from the high school band to help the organist on this day? And instead of doughnuts at the coffee hour, how about strawberries and cake?

One of the most distinctive observances for Whitsunday is easily arranged, namely the reading of the Gospel by several different people in several different languages. Even in small or isolated communities, there are always at least two or three people who know a foreign or ancient language. Some people whose mother tongue is not English will be deeply grateful for the opportunity to use their own language as part of an act of worship. The significance of this practice on Pentecost is so obvious as to require little explanation. In many cases, an interested lay person in the parish can assume the responsibility for identifying readers and securing the necessary Bibles a week or two in advance.

I recommend the following procedure for the actual liturgy. The traditional Pentecost story is read as usual. Then the priest can briefly announce that as we have heard about the proclamation of the Gospel in different tongues, so we will now enact it as an act of gratitude for the spreading of the Gospel through the world. The deacon or priest can then go to the place where the Gospel is to be read while an appropriate psalm or hymn is sung. (Try hymns 255, 256, 261, or 263 at this point.) At the same time the other appointed readers can come forward with their Bibles and stand near him. Then the deacon or priest can announce the Holy Gospel as usual and, after the *Gloria tibi,* read the appointed passage in English. Next, one of the other readers can proceed to read the same passage in another tongue, and then another, and so forth. The congregation will of course remain standing. The priest or the individual readers can announce which language it is before each reading. When the last one has finished, the response at the end of the Gospel, *Laus tibi,* can be said, and the liturgy proceeds as appointed. When a Pentecost Vigil is observed, a larger number of languages is easily included since the Gospel of the Vigil Eucharist is very brief.

One Whitsunday, the present writer was supplying in a small congregation in eastern Kansas. We had three languages, in addition to English, used for the Gospel. After the service, I asked one of the senior members of the congregation if he objected to the added length of the service. He shook his head, smiled, and said, "I wish we had had a dozen others."

It renews our realization of what the Gospel is when we are vividly reminded that it is *Good News* for "every tribe and tongue and people and nation."

VI

The Weeks after Pentecost

27:
The Other Half of the Year

Pentecost comes as the conclusion of the dramatic cycle which started half a year ago with Advent and Christmas, and then moved on through Lent, Easter, and Ascension Day. Whitsunday puts the finishing touches to that impressive series of church seasons.

After Trinity Sunday, everything suddenly becomes different. We begin a long series of quiet, ordinary Sundays which continue on through the other half of the Church Year. These two dozen "Green Sundays" are a challenge to us. What is the devout worshiper to make of them? What is to be done with them by clergy, choir leaders, and others involved in planning services of worship? What special significance can we find in them?

First of all, let us face the fact that this period is not really a season in the sense that Advent or Christmastide or Lent are seasons. Those shorter and more intense periods of the Church Year are each devoted to particular themes, and those themes are expressed in the Bible readings, psalms, prayers, and hymns of each season. It is evident that the series of weeks we have in the summer and fall simply do not constitute a season in that sense. The fact is that these summer and autumnal Sundays are just plain ordinary Sundays. They are designated numerically for convenience, because there is really no special doctrinal or theological sequence within them. So if you are looking for a seasonal theme, don't be confused or frustrated; no seasonal theme is there.

If this half of the year is not a season, then how are we to approach planning services and sermons? What principles or lines of approach should apply to the liturgy during these weeks? There is more than one answer. Special events or pastoral needs sometimes dictate a theme to be emphasized. Thus, because there are many weddings and wedding anniversaries in June, it is appropriate to have a sermon one Sunday on Christian marriage and to have prayers for married couples. Yet this should not be so strongly emphasized that bachelors and spinsters feel left out that week. Similarly, we usually have a more or less patriotic sermon on the Sunday nearest the Fourth of July—but neither should that be such that worshipers who belong to a different political party from the preacher feel they should have stayed home. On most of these Sundays, however, no such special topics are thrust upon us. What then will provide worshipers and clergy with some point of focus and unity? We would urge that *almost always* a theme should be taken from one or another of the Bible readings appointed for the day. This is, after all, the way the liturgy is constituted. The Bible is read soon after the service begins so that God's Word is heard first. It sets the stage for all that follows.

Most of the Gospel passages in this half year present our Lord's parables and miracles from his ministry in Galilee. They represent most of what we know about the ministry and teaching of Jesus. If the Church cannot concentrate on this for half a year, what can it do? The Epistles present doctrinal teaching, mostly from St. Paul. Again this is solid stuff. The Old Testament lessons usually have some relation to the Epistle or Gospel. All these passages have meanings which apply to us and our lives today.*

---

*For a valuable analysis of the contents of these readings Sunday by Sunday see A. Brooke Bushong, *A Guide to the Lectionary,* New York, Seabury Press, 1977.

28:
What Sunday Means

In the last essay we gave our attention to the primary liturgical fact of the summer, namely the occurrence of "just plain Sundays." These summer Sundays do not constitute a special season of the Church Year. They are simply ordinary Sundays. As thoughtful Christians, however, we may find that ordinary Sundays have extraordinary meaning. Every Sunday celebrates Creation, which the Bible associates with the first day of the week (Genesis 1:1–5). Every Sunday celebrates the Lord's Resurrection on the first day (Matthew 28:1ff.). Every Sunday celebrates the gift of the Holy Spirit which was manifest fifty days after the Resurrection at Pentecost (Acts 2:1–4, Leviticus 23:15–16).

The first Christians did not go to church on Sunday because it was a convenient public holiday. They assembled on the first day of the week (instead of Saturday, the Sabbath) because they wanted to celebrate the Resurrection. The manner and way that they celebrated it is what we call the liturgy. Passages from the Bible were read and preached about, and this "Ministry of the Word" came to be enclosed in a framework of praise and prayer. This first half of the service derived from the Jewish synagogue service. The second half of the liturgy derived from the Jewish practice of religious and ceremonial meals. Bread and wine were taken, a prayer of thanksgiving and consecration was said over them, the consecrated bread was broken up, the bread and wine were eaten and drunk.

The outline should be familiar to any Episcopalian. We are, perhaps, less familiar, however, with the way it was interpreted. The Bible readings were understood to express God's relationship to his whole creation, and also the new disclosure of himself given in the

Incarnation of his eternal Son. The Christian congregation and the Christian preacher, guided by the Holy Spirit, could interpret the whole Bible in the light of Christ—as the Lord himself taught his disciples to do on the first Easter (St. Luke 24:27, 44–48). Likewise, the second half of the liturgy, the "ministry of the Sacrament," was also seen in a "first day" sense. Modern Christians have tended to associate the Eucharist almost exclusively with the Last Supper. Ancient Christians associated it with the royal banquet of the parables, the wedding feast at Cana, the miraculous feedings, the meals our Savior had with his disciples after he rose from the dead (St. Luke 24:30, 41–43; St. John 21:12–13; Acts 10:41), and the anticipated wedding feast of heaven (Revelation 19:9). Thus, the Eucharist was seen very much in terms of the Resurrection.

The great Eucharistic Prayer, the long prayer of consecration said over the bread and wine, seems to have developed very much as a Sunday prayer. After the *Sursum corda*, praise and thanksgiving are offered to God our Creator, then we worship him for sending his Son to redeem us, and we pray for the action of the Holy Spirit in the sacrament and in the Church.

The act of breaking the bread again is strongly associated with the Resurrection and Pentecost by Luke in his Gospel (24:30–31, 35) and in Acts (2:42, 46). The paschal associations of the breaking of the bread were recognized by Archbishop Cranmer in the Mass in his first English Prayer Book of 1549. Immediately after the Lord's Prayer (the traditional place for the breaking) he introduced the words "Christ our paschal Lamb is offered up for us . . . wherefore let us keep a joyful and holy feast with the Lord." This is a free quotation from St. Paul, I Corinthians 5:7–8.

All these levels of meaning are summed up at the time of our Communion as we receive into our souls the risen Christ, who is "the image of the invisible God, the first-born of all creation" (Colossians 1:15), "the first-born from the dead" (Colossians 1:18), and the one through whom the Holy Spirit is sent to those who believe in him (Acts 2).*

Our Hymnal does have many familiar hymns expressing the

trinitarian meaning of Sunday. These include 267, 271, 272, 274, 275, and 474. Gentle reader, do not opt for all of these in one week. If one such hymn is used every week or two, and accompanied by some explanation, some helpful teaching can be imparted. Usually, all these themes will not be expressed in one hymn, nor will they all be explained in one sermon. Throughout the summer, those who are responsible for choosing hymns and for preparing sermons can ask themselves whether the great themes of Creation, Resurrection, and new life in the Spirit are being touched on regularly and consistently. At the very least, this is a way of checking the compass and making sure that we are theologically sailing a straight course.

Of course none of us spends the whole day in church. Because Sunday is always a feast, it is right for Christians to spend much of the day enjoying themselves. In recreation we can experience both the beauty of God's creation and the good things of human culture. Christians have always believed it to be an appropriate day to practice hospitality and to eat and drink with friends. Enjoying life on the Lord's Day, we know that earthly existence is not meaningless or futile—neither is it final or ultimate. God has prepared something better for those who love him.

---

*For a helpful analysis of the normal pattern of eucharistic celebration on Sunday, see *Parish Eucharist*, The Associated Parishes, Inc., 1977.

29:
The Liturgy of Marriage

June continues to be an important time for weddings, and the arrangements and planning of the service deserve careful thought. Within a particular congregation, a parish worship committee can establish certain guidelines which can be helpful both to the clergy and to prospective couples. Of course, every wedding is different. Individual preferences, local customs, the size and shape of the church are among the factors to be considered in planning a wedding. In a church wedding, however, the historical liturgical tradition should certainly be neither the last nor the least of the factors considered.

Our Episcopal churches provide a uniquely beautiful setting for weddings. Yet too often in the past we contented ourselves with a four and one-half page service, with no Bible readings, no hymns, few prayers, and no sacramental use of the altar. How does that relate to liturgy or to the Anglican emphasis on the Word of God and the sacraments of the Gospel?

Historically, Christian marriages were solemnized in the context of the Eucharist. For centuries, the so-called Nuptial Mass had appropriate Collect, Epistle, Gospel, etc. The bride and groom kissed each other at the Peace, and received Holy Communion together. The early English Books of Common Prayer required that the wedding service be followed by the Eucharist, including a sermon or homily, and the reception of Holy Communion by the couple. This was later reduced to a rubric stating that it was "convenient that the new married persons should receive the holy Communion." Even this good advice disappeared from our American editions of the Prayer Book.

Our 1928 Prayer Book began the work of restoring the tradition of the liturgical wedding with the provision of a proper Collect, Epistle, and Gospel for use at a nuptial celebration of the Eucharist. In the Proposed Book of Common Prayer the arrangement of the marriage service continues the thrust of the 1928 revision by printing out the integration of the two services, with the first promises at the beginning, then the Ministry of the Word, then the solemn vows, prayers, blessing, and the Peace. If the Eucharist is to be celebrated, it continues with the Offertory. The Nuptial Eucharist is encouraged. If it is not celebrated (and sometimes it is neither appropriate nor desirable), the service is still a complete act of Christian worship, with Scripture reading, several prayers, and congregational responses. Psalmody, hymns, and homily, if desired, are appointed at suitable places.

Enhanced congregational participation can be readily planned, especially if there is a Communion. A friend or relative can read the Old Testament Lesson or Epistle. A deacon, an additional priest, or a minister of another denomination can be given appropriate parts. (A parish worship committee can make it known that by inviting more than one clergyman to participate in the wedding service, the groom is not obligating himself to give gratuities to each of them.) The couple can present the bread and wine at the altar at the Offertory—sometimes the bride has made the bread herself. Friends or relatives can serve as acolytes. In some cases, an usher who knows how to serve can go up to the altar to help the priest for the Offertory and the ablutions. The question of how many members of the wedding party will receive Holy Communion can be discussed with them beforehand. A parish worship committee can consider some policy as to how "open" the reception of Holy Communion should be at weddings. If a discreet announcement is made at the service, inviting those "who are prepared and desirous" to receive the Sacrament, people who do not share our sacramental beliefs are usually sensitive and courteous enough to understand that this is their cue not to come forward.

A bigger question is "Why?" What is the purpose of having the

Holy Eucharist at the main wedding service? If the bride and groom happen to wish to receive Holy Communion, why can't they do so in the quiet and privacy of an "early service?" The answer to this question requires long-term teaching. The Eucharist celebrates the very things that Christian marriage is all about: the personal involvement of God, through the incarnation of his Son, in the flesh-and-blood reality of human life; sacrifice as both the expression and the foundation of love; and the union between Christ and his Church as something in which the husband and wife participate.

Today, many marriages are shaky and many families are deeply troubled. Good liturgy by itself will not make this problem go away. Where other constructive pastoral factors are at work, good liturgy should support and confirm Christian marriage. June is not only a time for weddings, but also an appropriate time for a positive sermon or two on the subject of matrimony at the Sunday morning services. Suitable prayers for married couples may be added to the Prayers of the People. Within the marriage service there are several suitable prayers to choose from. In terms of the personal lives of our people, is not the reestablishment of the stability of marriage perhaps the major pastoral challenge facing the Church today?

30:
Lesser Holy Days

If one looks at the Episcopal calendars now commonly in use, including the one in the front of the Proposed Book of Common Prayer, for each month one finds about a dozen names in small type or black type, in addition to the few names in large type or printed in red. The large type or red letter days indicate festivals which are supposed to be observed throughout the Episcopal Church. At Morning or Evening Prayer, or at a celebration of the Eucharist, the assigned readings for the day are to be used. It is generally understood that at parish churches with a resident priest, the Eucharist should be celebrated on all such red letter days, or else the observance should be held on some other day of that week. The somewhat complicated factors involved in transferring such days are discussed above in Essay 10.

Let us consider the so-called lesser feasts, the ones usually indicated in smaller type or black letters. We do not, properly speaking, refer to the people so listed as lesser saints, for who are we to judge? St. Augustine of Hippo (August 28), for instance, has apparently had a far greater influence on Christian history than the Apostle Bartholomew (August 24). But we do speak of St. Augustine, among many others, as having a "lesser feast" because the customary liturgical commemoration is less than that traditionally accorded to the apostles. It would be quite impossible to provide equally great commemorations for all the heroes of Christian history.

To judge how many greater and lesser days should occupy our calendar is a difficult task, and the number of such observances has been increased or decreased from time to time in the course of history. Geographic considerations also influence church calendars. No doubt St. Augustine's day is regarded as a major feast in North Africa where he lived. (This Augustine is not to be confused with Augustine of Canterbury whom we commemorate on May 26. The latter is, of course, a major festival in Canterbury Cathedral.) Conversely, among Eastern Orthodox Christians, the name of Augustine is not revered at all. Within the Anglican Communion, the red letter days are almost the same all over the world, but the black letter days vary, to some extent, in our different national Churches. The Scottish Book of Common Prayer, for instance, includes many ancient Scottish saints whose names are unknown to American Episcopalians. On the other hand, we have certain names that are historically and devotionally important for the American Church, such as William Augustus Muhlenberg (April 8), John Henry Hobart (September 12), Samuel Seabury (November 14). Are these latter really "saints"? The question is not so readily answered. The title of saint goes easily with biblical, ancient, or medieval names, but it sounds a bit strange with a modern American name such as, say, "Saint Wilbur McCorkle Smith, Jr." In the course of Christian history, heroes have often been held in honor for centuries before the title of saint became formally attributed to them. Let us leave it that way. We can comfortably speak of Dr. Muhlenburg, Bishop Hobart, or Bishop Seabury. Later centuries of history can add other titles if they feel moved to do so.

Meanwhile what are we supposed to do with these lesser days? First of all, throughout the Anglican Communion such lesser days are optional. We do not have to do anything with them. We believe it valuable and significant to affirm our spiritual roots and heritage by having them in the calendar, but we are not obliged to have any special public celebrations of them. When they land on a Sunday, their observance is not usually permitted. For the daily services of Morning and Evening Prayer, they do not have special psalms or lessons assigned to them; if they had, it would totally disrupt the sequence of daily readings. An appropriate Collect may be used if desired. In some cases, a particular opening sentence or canticle may also be appropriate. Suitable Collects may be found in the Proposed Prayer Book, pages 195–199 and 246–250. A simpler commemoration is made possible in the evening with the short litany, which may be used before the Collects, pages 68 and 122. Here the name can simply be inserted in the final clause. For celebrations of the Eucharist, optional readings are provided in the lectionary, since there is normally no sequence of readings from day to day for weekday celebrations, and Proper Prefaces may be used. Some parishes prefer to use white or red vestments for the days they observe, others prefer to retain the color of the week. It certainly is not necessary for the altar guild to change the frontal, pulpit cloth, and lectern bookmarks for every lesser feast. On the other hand, they may wish to do so for certain of these days that are felt to have extra importance. On a number of black letter days, the figure commemorated is associated with some particular topic or theme which may be appropriately expressed in the intercessions at the Eucharist or in the concluding prayers of the daily offices. Thus on the day of St. Benedict of Nursia (July 11) we may pray for the Benedictine monks and nuns, or for all monastic communities. On William Wilberforce's day (July 30), we may pray for the continuing abolition of slavery in all parts of the world.

For members of the Episcopal Church, perhaps the most useful observance of these days is to follow the excellent book, *Lesser Feasts and Fasts,* Revised Edition (1974). Here there is a Collect which can be said on each of these days, and in the latter part of the book is a short but informative biographical sketch of each figure. These can be read by individuals or families in their private devotions, and can be read publicly at weekday services. Those following this book through the year will be tremendously profited in their knowledge of the faith and history of the Church, and in their personal awareness of the communion of saints.

A special case arises in a church named for one of these saints or heroes. The patronal feast is always a major celebration for the church involved. A parish dedicated to St. Benedict will wish to celebrate his feast in the fullest way, and in many cases will wish to do so on the following Sunday. The lectionary for the daily offices provide suitable psalms and lessons, so that a patronal feast can be observed on the preceding evening, and at Morning and Evening Prayer of the day, as well as at celebrations of the Holy Eucharist.

31:
The Gift of Summer

The "Good Old Summer Time" is with us again. These are the days for baseball, swimming, and eating out-of-doors. Summer is a time for families to be together, a time for long evenings when one can sit on the porch and talk, a time for sweet corn, iced tea, and fresh peaches. Summer is not the time for committee meetings and all the scheduled activities which keep many of us so busy during the winter.

Where does this leave the parish church during July and August? Some churches butt their heads against the summer and attempt, successfully or unsuccessfully, to maintain the sort of schedule they have in the winter. Instead of fighting the summer, why not join it? Summer is a great season for churches to do certain things which they cannot do in the winter. We can have services and activities that reflect enjoyment of what summer is. Birds and flowers and blue skys are gifts of God, and Catholic Christians ought to take the doctrine of creation seriously.

Worship can be less formal, less heavy-handed, more open in spirit so that young and old can participate fully. If your parish has its main service earlier on Sunday morning in the summer, and if the choir has folded up for the season, that does not mean that you and your fellow worshipers need to be confined to a routine type of "early service." Have simpler, informal music that everyone can sing. If your church has a large chancel, let everyone be invited up to sit together in the choir stalls. Priests do not always have to look so overheated in all those vestments. A voluminous chasuble of inexpensive, unlined cotton print can easily be made by a needle-wise parishioner, and it can be worn over a priest's shirtsleeves.

Everyone will feel better when the priest looks cooler.

Some congregations, with unairconditioned churches in warm parts of the country, would do better to go downstairs to the undercroft for their main Sunday service. Let some talented parishioners arrange a sanctuary and decorate it with colored paper, painted cardboard, cloth, or whatever they choose. In any case, it won't be permanent and everyone can enjoy something different for several weeks.

What about an occasional service out-of-doors? If you are in the country or the suburbs, is there a large shady tree near your church where you can gather around a temporary altar? If you are in the city can you arrange to have a service in a park? People at summer camps and conferences have always known the great impression out-of-doors services can make. Why can't the people who are in the parish at home have a similar experience? The best thing of all is to arrange a baptism at a pond or river or seashore site. This can be followed by an out-of-door Eucharist and parish picnic. This can be one of the high points of the year.

At a conference on the Church in the summer held at Roanridge some time ago, we were amazed at the variety of constructive and enjoyable things different congregations reported doing. One parish in a small Missouri town concentrated its summer program on two things: the Sunday morning service and a midweek evening service. For the latter, each week a different family invited the congregation to meet in their backyard. They had an informal out-of-door Eucharist, followed by a cookout supper. Then there was an event for the children (a game, project, or learning activity of some type) and a group discussion, movie, or other informal program for the adults. Sometimes people just sat around after supper and talked for an hour or two and enjoyed something cool to drink. Many ideas were exchanged, and many friendships formed. The whole parish, for the whole rest of the year, was stronger because of the long happy evenings which families shared together. What use does your parish plan to make of the gift of summer?

32:
Church in Vacation Time

In the last essay we considered some of the creative and constructive things parish churches can do during the time of the year when much of the congregation is away on vacation. But what about those people who are away? When you and I go away for a weekend or for a longer period, what do we do about our obligations to worship God on Sunday?

Perhaps Episcopalians would make greater efforts to attend church when away from home if we were all aware of how encouraging it is to any church to have vacationing visitors join the congregation. What a lift it gives to people going into church to see a family pull up in a dusty car with a license plate from across the nation! And it may also stimulate us and widen our own vision to worship in a congregation a little different from our parish back home. We may even get some new ideas which may benefit our own church.

But sometimes we go to places where there isn't a church, or at least not a church we can easily worship in. What then? The writer confesses to having been rather fortunate in this regard. For many years my family and I have visited a small island on the seacoast where there is no Episcopal church, but there is a Methodist church where a community-church type of service is held on Sunday evenings. Fifteen years ago, my family and some other families felt that there was no reason why we should not have the sacramental worship of our own Church. Accordingly, we began to have, with the permission of the bishop of the diocese, a simple celebration of the Eucharist every Sunday morning. The Methodist church very hospitably invited us to use its facilities for this purpose. Over the years, this service has been welcomed by many summer people and also a few residents of the island. Thus, a small worshiping congregation has come into existence without cost to the diocese and without involving anyone in administrative responsibilities that no one desires to take on during their summer vacation.

We have continued to work cooperatively with the Methodist pastor, and many Episcopalians have been actively involved in different parts of his program. We do not have a large Episcopal congregation. Precisely because it is small and somewhat informal, it provides a dimension of worship which is valued by people who during the winter attend nothing but a large urban or suburban parish. Opportunities for different worshipers to take turns reading lessons, leading the intercessions, or collecting the alms and bringing forward the elements, have been welcomed. Families and friends worshiping together in this kind of setting can offer to God in worship the kind of experience which their summer vacation represents.

This example is not typical, in the sense that not every family includes within it a priest. On the other hand, this example *is* typical in the sense that a large number of communities located on seashores, lakes, or mountains, where many people go during the summer, are in fact often visited by Episcopal clergy. The truth is that visiting clergy are shy about conducting services if no one invites them to, and lay people are shy about asking priests to officiate in places where they are only temporary visitors. Dioceses are shy about encouraging summer congregations because they fear financial and administrative involvement. Do not some of our attitudes require reexamination?

In any case, members of the Church can certainly worship even if a clergyman is not available. Several years ago a vestryman of a substantial parish acquired deserved fame. He and his family were very regular churchgoers, but at a certain point he purchased a cottage on a lake in the country and began to go there with his family for weekends in summer. They felt they should do something about worship, so they began reading Morning Prayer together every Sunday morning in their cottage. A neighboring family soon discovered what they were doing and asked to join them. A week or two later another family asked if they might participate. By the end of the summer, a small congregation had developed. During the winter the vestryman told his rector about this, and he suggested that our friend study for the diocesan lay reader's license, which he did. Thus, a small summer congregation came into existence under the leadership of this layman. Plans were subsequently made so that a priest could come from time to time in the summer to celebrate the Eucharist.

Every weekend during the summer untold thousands of Americans visit national parks in various parts of our nation. The National Park Service does not itself have any chaplaincy. Most of the larger parks, however, do have some arrangements for Christian worship on Sunday. In most cases, these have been arranged and organized by the agency called A Christian Ministry in the National Parks (ACMNP). This is a very ecumenical organization to which the Episcopal Church contributes some support, and which cooperates very closely with the Episcopal Church in certain localities.

The personnel of ACMNP are mostly students who are recruited during the winter from theological schools and seminaries. ACMNP arranges placement for them in parks during the summer and secures for them positions working in hotels, restaurants, and other enterprises within the parks. Thus, they support themselves by secular work, with the understanding that they will have sufficient free time to arrange church services on Sundays and on some other occasions, and to serve as chaplains to the large number of other young persons who have summer jobs in the parks and who in many cases have personal needs and problems. ACMNP has been one of the real pioneers in the United States in utilizing the worker-priest or nonstipendiary minister concept. Learning something about this creative and unique organization may add to the interest of worshiping together with other Christians who are on vacation the next time you are in Yellowstone or Yosemite or some other national park. National parks are not all in the West, however, and

ACMNP has personnel working in locations from the Virgin Islands to Alaska. America still has a lot of space out-of-doors, and the out-of-doors can still teach you and me something about the power and transcendence of our Creator.

33:
St. Mary in the Liturgy

It is one of the many ironies of religious history that the saint who is recognized as unique by all Christians should have become an object of bitter contention. Such is the case with Our Lord's Blessed Mother. The ancient Eastern Orthodox and Western Catholic liturgies generally have frequent and very honorific references to St. Mary. At the time of the Reformation, in the sixteenth century, Protestants were generally eager to remove or minimize such references. As usual, the Church of England pursued a middle path. In the historic editions of the Book of Common Prayer, she is, of course, referred to constantly in the creeds. At Morning Prayer her role in the Incarnation is alluded to in the *Te Deum* (in traditional Anglican practice this was said or sung daily except in Lent) and in the evening in the *Magnificat.* In the calendar, she is conspicuous in the Christmas-Epiphany period. The Feast of the Presentation of our Lord or the Purification of St. Mary, traditionally known in England as Candlemas (February 2), is associated with her, as is the Annunciation (March 25), formerly widely known among Anglicans as Lady Day. On the other hand, the historic English Prayer Books did not retain several medieval feasts specifically in honor of Mary. The most notable of such omissions was her feast on August 15, generally regarded in the Middle Ages as the date of her assumption, or passage up to heaven. The modern Roman Catholic belief that she was bodily taken up into heaven has seemed superstitious and offensive to most non-Roman Western Christians, and has not commended this feast.

Yet a problem has remained for Anglicans. On the one hand, we observe red letter feasts for most other major New Testament figures, including such obscure apostles as St. Bartholomew or St. Jude. Yet we deny such a feast to the person most responsible, at the human level, for our Lord's birth into this world. True, she is commemorated at Christmas, Candlemas, and the Annunciation, but, as has frequently been pointed out, these are really feasts of our Lord, and the Annunciation is often displaced and obscured by Holy Week or Easter. In short, there has been good reason to restore that feast on August 15 which has been St. Mary's Day since early Christian times. The association with the doctrine of the assumption was a later addition which does not involve Episcopalians.

Fifteen years ago when the Standing Liturgical Commission was restoring the calendar of lesser feasts in the Episcopal Church, this Feast of St. Mary was hesitantly put forward. It was feared that it would be seized on as an object of controversy. In fact this did not happen. Episcopalians, if they were concerned about the question at all, accepted this addition to the calendar in the amicable and noncontroversial spirit that was intended. The same was true of the Feast of the Visitation (May 31). A few years later, as plans began to be made for a revision of the Prayer Book, these days were reconsidered. The Visitation is really a feast of our Lord and thus, if observed at all, should be a red letter day. Similarly, if our Lord's Mother is recognized as a major New Testament figure, then according to our prevailing Anglican system, she should, like the others, have a red letter day for which no special explanations are needed. For the same reason, it may be noted, the red letter status of St. Mary Magdalene's observance (July 22) was restored.

Falling in midsummer, we cannot suppose that St. Mary's Day will become a major event in the life of most parishes. On the other hand, we should give it as much emphasis as can appropriately be given to a weekday observance. It certainly should be publicly announced. For too many other Christians, both Catholic and Protestant, our Lord's Mother is still a topic for quarreling. We Anglicans have a valuable witness to offer in our ability to honor St. Mary without worshiping her, and to uphold her unique place in the history of salvation without adding unscriptural and unsuitable elaborations.

Meanwhile, the historic Anglican daily use of the *Te Deum* and *Magnificat* has had little impact in modern America, where few church people hear these said or sung, even on Sundays. The Proposed Prayer Book compensates for this, in a sense, by including references to the Incarnation in Eucharistic Prayers, and in two of them specifically naming the Virgin Mary. Similarly, two of the intercessions, Form V (page 391) and the conclusion of Eucharistic Prayer D (page 375), permit the custom of regularly naming her among the saints. Such specificity is desirable within liturgical formulations. A phrase like "the communion of saints" loses its meaning if one does not frequently hear of real and specific individual saints. Similarly, the word "incarnation" is very orthodox, but when this term stands by itself, it is rather technical and intellectual. On the other hand, when a prayer goes on to speak of Jesus being born of the Virgin Mary, it suggests the wonder and mystery of the Son of God entering human flesh through the motherhood of a young Jewish woman. Liturgy must speak to the heart as well as to the head; it must gather up body, mind, and spirit, and for this reason must be suggestive, evocative, and artistic as well as reasonable.

34:
Prayer in the Morning

During fall, winter, and spring, we are very much aware of formal public religious activities—the opening of Sunday school, Advent, Christmas, Lent, Easter. In the summer we are thrown more on our own. This is not a bad thing. Public and corporate church life should nourish our individual spirituality. Similarly, our own personal experience as believing, perceiving, and praying Christians should bring vitality and strength to the collective life of the Church.

For many individuals, one of the great spiritual opportunities of the summer is for prayer in the morning. There are innumerable ways to pray in the morning or any other time, and what suits you may be unique. Episcopalians have generally found, however, a special value in using the traditional office of the Church—Daily Morning Prayer. Summer is a good time to reexplore this part of our spiritual heritage. Here we are speaking of Daily Morning Prayer as a relatively brief pattern of psalms, Bible readings, canticles, and prayers appropriate for individuals or groups to use at the beginning of the day. This has always been provided in the various editions of our Prayer Book. Some people only know it as a more elaborate service, to which choir procession, anthem, sermon, and so forth, have been added, as used at a late hour on Sunday morning. Some clergy think of this service as they recall it at a seminary or other institution, in which it served as "school prayers" and was led by faculty members in academic attire. These and other developments represent possible options within our tradition. The present discussion, however, is directed at the plain, simple, basic sense of the service: daily prayer in the morning.

Worship in the morning, before the phone has begun to ring and before the hustle and bustle of daily life has engulfed our consciousness, is a distinct kind of experience. It may be difficult in winter, for dragging ourselves from bed to face a dark and cold day is not one of life's most gratifying experiences. In July, on the other hand, it is easy to enjoy the hour before breakfast. The blue sky, the clean fresh air, and the sparkle of dewdrops draw us to the open window or onto the porch or out into the backyard or patio. We can recognize light, clouds, buildings, trees, birds, and the ground beneath us as gifts that have been given to us. We can recognize our own reawakening consciousness as a new and fresh installment of the gift of life itself. In short, we can perceive something of the mystery of our createdness, the wonder of being upheld in the hand of our Maker. Of course, not every morning is ideal, but the wonder of our existence and the beauty of the world of which we are a part, are indeed there awaiting us. This kind of perception is at the heart of Christian worship in the morning. Our Anglican type of morning office is really about this—if we can forget the preludes, the academic hoods, and the processions, and turn our thoughts instead to the rising sun.

If we can get hold of this vision, or, rather, let this vision get hold of us, then such familiar elements of Morning Prayer as the *Venite*, *Te Deum*, Apostles' Creed and Lord's Prayer are illuminated in a new way. Stated more theologically, by the power of the Holy Spirit the Christian worshiper perceives creation in the light of the Resurrection.

We are not suggesting that the morning is the only time one can or should have such an experience. Nor is it being suggested that this is the only theme of importance in the morning service. We are suggesting, rather, that this kind of experience can make an important contribution to our own personal spirituality and that the early morning is certainly a time when such an experience can be accessible to many people.

To me, a very helpful expression of this is in the beautiful modern English hymn by Eleanor Farjeon:

> Morning has broken
> like the first morning,
> Blackbird has spoken
> like the first bird . . .

A similar outlook is implicit in the great Collect for the morning derived from a collection of prayers by William Reed Huntington:

> O God, the King eternal, who dividest the day from the night and turnest the shadow of death into the morning . . .

(Proposed Prayer Book, pages 56 and 99)

It is not enough, however, for such a prayer to be printed in books: it is the thoughtful, reflective, and repeated use of such devotions which matters. May such worship open for us the door to new understandings of the mystery of the morning, and of the mystery of life.

So, good reader, begin tomorrow by taking your Bible and Prayer Book, going to the open window or back porch, and reciting the morning service. Perhaps your husband or wife will wish to join you. If no one has ever explained to you how to find the appointed psalms and Bible readings, then simply begin by using ones you like. In due course, you will get the hang of it. If the whole service is too long for you, use half of it. With practice it becomes easier to find the places and proceed with less delay. On the other hand, speed is not the goal. One of the beauties of reciting the service privately in the summer is that one can take time and be unhurried. You may wish to reflect several minutes on a Bible passage, or add several extra prayers at the end. By all means do so. On certain days, there may be things of special importance to you that you wish to pray about. By all means do this too. When this service is used privately, it is a mixture of the corporate concerns of the Church as a whole and the individual concerns of the worshiper. This too is as it should be. We find our own fullest personhood within the fellowship of Christ's body. Likewise, the Church corporately lives in and through the life of its many members.

35:
Back-to-School Month

Because so many young people are fortunately attending schools, and because there are so many parents, the beginning of the school year touches most of us. It certainly makes itself felt in church, with the hustle and bustle after the quiet summer months. New faces suddenly appear in church and in Sunday school, and many old faces reappear. Will the services of worship and other activities and programs of the church respond to this opportunity? Will they fulfill the expectations of those who are beginning the year with such hope and enthusiasm?

In most parishes it is well understood that Sunday school matters must be well planned in advance. Similarly, parish organizations and social events follow a schedule to which some thought has been devoted. But what about that most conspicuous and well-known activity of the local church, namely worship on Sunday morning? What sort of planning has been devoted to that in preparation for the opportunities offered by September?

As has been said before, we do not regard midsummer as an ideal time for committee meetings, but some preliminary planning has got to be done. The meeting of a worship committee in August need not be an unpleasant event. It can be scheduled for a midweek evening and can be open to all interested members of the congregation. It can include discussion of a number of items to be dealt with and a suitable act of worship, such as the Order of Worship for the Evening, Evening Prayer, Compline, or a celebration of the Eucharist. It is good for the committee to worship together as well as to talk about worship, and this is a good opportunity for the committee to experience new or old forms of worship with which they may not be familiar. Later on, cheese, beer, iced tea, or other suitable refreshments can be served. In the convivial atmosphere of a summer night, some very good theological discussions can arise.

Being prepared for September does not necessarily mean that a rigid schedule of services must be adopted at this time and followed without change until the next June. On the contrary, some changes during the course of the coming months may be anticipated and intended. The introduction of more music into the liturgy, or more extensive use of lay readers, may be projected over a period of time and developed step by step. On the other hand, in worship as in other matters, good quality requires serious commitment to the discipline of planning. For instance, if after due consideration it has been decided that it is possible and desirable to reintroduce Evensong on Sunday afternoon, one should not abandon the plan simply because attendance is small for the first few weeks. It may require several months for a new service in the parish schedule to establish itself. Many positive and constructive steps are only possible if planning has taken place. If some new types of music are to be used, this may require research, study, and perhaps practice with some other musician in another church on the part of the organist or choir director. This cannot be done on a few days' notice. Similarly it is unjust to musicians to encourage such development of new skills, perhaps at some cost to themselves, and then never give them appropriate opportunity to utilize the new material. Likewise, the sudden and relatively unexpected assignment of important liturgical responsibilities to lay readers can be a disaster for all concerned. On the other hand, many a lay reader could preach an excellent original sermon on, for instance, the Second Sunday of Advent if this was unequivocally assigned to the reader in late October.

It is obvious that the most effective parochial program of worship should be coordinated with arrangements for Christian education and other activities and events. Coordination cannot take place without a number of people making the effort to look into the future.

36:
St. Luke's Day
and Ministry to the Sick

October, like other months, has its fair share of major and minor saints' days. One of the major ones is, of course, St. Luke's Day on October 18. As the author of one of the Gospels and also of the Acts of the Apostles, Luke is justly loved. His day also has another dimension. The Epistle to the Colossians (4:14) calls Luke "the beloved physician," and it has been generally assumed that this indicates the profession of the writer of the Gospel. Hence, during the recent past it has become customary in our churches to have prayers for hospitals and for doctors, nurses, and medical workers on this day or on the Sunday preceding or following. This practice has much to commend it. Let us consider some possible amplifications and variations.

First of all, the ministry of the Church to the sick is certainly a topic deserving at least one sermon per year. The Sunday before or after St. Luke's Day is one time for it. It can be a solidly instructional, or teaching, sermon. There are certain things people should be asked to hear about and to think about when they are in good health, for when they are sick, or perhaps dying, it may be too late. This is also a good time of year for clergy and parish leaders to ask themselves about the long-range goals of the parish in ministering to the sick. In many areas, there is a prayer group especially concerned with praying for the sick. A further step is to provide training for several responsible persons to undertake visiting the sick in behalf of the Church, praying with them and, on appropriate occasions, accompanying the priest when the Eucharist is to be administered in a home or hospital room. The ordained clergy themselves continue to have a unique responsibility for sacramental ministrations to the sick. Here again there is an open season for teaching. The procedures for Communion from the reserved Sacrament, or for a brief celebration at the bedside, are quite unknown to most Episcopalians. It is often said nowadays that sickness should not be viewed as a punishment for sin. Yet many people do have serious reasons for guilt, and illness remains a significant opportunity for self-examination, penitence, and confession.

Least known to most people is anointing or unction (both words mean the same thing). Ordinary pure olive oil is used for anointing the sick, but prior to use it is blessed and set apart for its sacramental purpose. Our 1928 Prayer Book gave no information at all relative to such blessing. The present Proposed Prayer Book (page 455) gives a form of words for the blessing, but no suggestions for the manner of carrying it out. The simplest procedure, which is probably widespread in the Episcopal Church, is for the priest to recite the blessing over a small container of oil immediately prior to use in the sick room. What remains is then used on other occasions without any subsequent blessing. The alternate approach is to bless a substantial quantity of oil from time to time at a general service of public worship in church. This provides everyone with the opportunity to unite their prayers with those of the priest in behalf of all who may, at any future time, be anointed with this oil. It also provides everyone with an opportunity to be made aware of this rite and gain some understanding of it.

Within the Roman rite, which is in so many respects the ancestor of our own, it has been the practice for over a thousand years to have the oil for the sick blessed by the bishop on Maundy Thursday, at the same Mass that the oil for catechumens and the chrism for the newly baptized are blessed. It is a very long and complicated service, the different parts of which have not always been well understood. Anglican adaptations of this rite usually leave much to be desired.

Participants have not always clearly known which oil was being blessed for which purposes. In any case, on Maundy Thursday, the thoughts of the Church are properly given over to the Lord's Passion, and the oil for the sick will receive at best a few moments' attention. If unction of the sick is to be given a place of proper dignity, the public blessing of this oil surely must take place at some other time or times.

We are here suggesting that St. Luke's Day, or the Sunday before or after it, is a very suitable occasion, at least in our present period of liturgical history. There is no need to restrict this blessing to the bishop, although, of course, he should perform it if present. The presence of the bishop on this occasion is especially appropriate in the chapel of a Church-affiliated hospital, or in some parish that has an especially active ministry to the sick. When, as is more likely to be the case, a priest officiates at the blessing of this oil, he need not do so in an unduly elaborate or pretentious manner. It is interesting to note, however, that the rites of the sick are the only sacramental functions specifically entrusted to priests or presbyters in the New Testament (see the Epistle of St. James 5:14–16).

How is such a public blessing best carried out? Although it could be quite legitimately performed at the conclusion of the public recitation of one of the daily offices, tradition strongly favors the Eucharist as the context for such a blessing. If some sick people are to be attending the service and are to be publicly anointed in church, the rubric in the Proposed Prayer Book, page 453, would indicate that the blessing of the oil take place no later than just before the exchange of the Peace. At that point, someone can bring forward the container of oil to be blessed, perhaps on a small silver tray, and it can be placed on the altar. It will be appropriate if someone who has been specially associated with the care or ministry to the sick do this. The officiating bishop or priest can then lay a hand upon the open container and recite the prayer of blessing. If additional priests are present, they too can appropriately extend their hands over the oil being blessed. In the past, it has been customary for such oil to be contained in a small silver vessel, slightly larger than a thimble, known as an oil stock. Such a small container is hardly suitable at a public ceremony, as it can only be seen by the few people who are standing nearby.

37:
The Festival of All God's Saints

All through October, local shops and neighborhood stores will be amassing their collection of paper and cardboard pumpkins, black cats, skeletons, witches' hats, and so forth. A great deal of preparation goes into sustaining Hallowe'en as one of the great American folk festivals. The next morning, in too many cases, the solemnity of All Saints will be marked by a mere handful of people gathering with their rector at a side altar. In many parishes, the majority of the people are scarcely even aware that the day has come and gone. We are not suggesting that this festival be commercialized, or that it be the object of the Church's entire promotional effort during the preceding weeks. We are suggesting that some constructive planning and preparation can take place, and that this feast can be very rewarding, both for the parish and for the individual worshiper.

All Saints' Day is not among the most ancient Christian festivals (it is only about 1200 years old), nor among the most universal (the Greeks commemorate all the saints at the time of Pentecost). The feast is believed to have been originated in the British Isles, and emphasis on it remains characteristically Anglican. We believe it none the worse for that. It expresses, as no individual saints' days can, the total communion of saints, and the corporate realization of salvation in that heavenly country "where there shall be no more mourning nor crying nor pain any more" (Revelation 21:4). As both the agricultural year and the ecclesiastical year come to an end, there is something especially moving in this celebration of the end of time itself, and of the harvest of all human history.

Some parishes have a potluck supper on Hallowe'en, together

with some suitable activities for young people. Recent crimes and tragedies connected with trick-or-treat expeditions have made such a supervised program desirable in many communities. It may include, among other possibilities, trick-or-treating in a very few nearby selected sites, or a visit to a "haunted house," or prizes for the best costumes. Such a program can conclude back at the church with a service of worship. Planning such a service offers many creative opportunities, and in some parishes this has become a major event. The next day the Eucharist will no doubt be celebrated at what is hoped will be a convenient hour—although in many places it seems almost impossible to find a convenient hour on a working day. Even where a goodly number of people do come on Hallowe'n or November 1, most parishes will also wish a major observance on the Sunday following. The Proposed Prayer Book allows this and conveniently provides two complete sets of propers, page 925, so that people who have observed the feast during the week will not be faced with precisely the same set of readings the following Sunday.

This Sunday can be a splendid occasion. The "Saints' Days" section of our Hymnal contains some very stirring hymns. Others occur among the final twenty numbers of the Hymnal. Every parish, whether it be large or small, ritualistic or austere, can do what it does to observe a great feast. It is a time for the best vestments, extra candles, banners, and flowers. Most of us have not had all that since last spring and it will be welcome at this time. There should be the fullest participation by acolytes, lay readers, and additional clergy if any are available. The new liturgy proposes this as an occasion for administering Holy Baptism (page 312), and for many years some parishes have successfully maintained this as the one time in the fall for baptisms at the main Sunday service. It can be baptism with all the trimmings, including the decoration of the font with flowers and candles, and a liturgical procession in which sponsors and candidates take part. If there are nonparochial or retired priests or deacons in your parish, consider inviting them on this day to take part in the celebration of Holy Baptism and the Eucharist. Baptism on this day dramatizes an aspect of the meaning of all baptisms as incorporation into the Body of Christ, which is the Holy Catholic Church, the communion of saints, a fellowship of the Holy Spirit encompassing the living and the dead, extending from the remote past on into the future when the Lord will come again to make all things new.

All Saints' Day merits being treated differently from other saints' days, for the others come and go, usually with little public observance. In some cases, it is simply impossible to have more than a small number of people take part in the liturgical rites of these days. The result has been that the very awareness of saints' days is dim for many people, and the purpose of such an observance is obscure. Compensating in some measure for the disregard of the other days, All Saints' Day can be strongly emphasized in every parish, and treated as a major festival each fall. As with other liturgical observances, a full understanding of it requires time and repetition. Holy days build up a context of memories and associations by being celebrated year after year. You can have a better observance next year if you have a good observance this year.

38:
Remembering the Dead

The commemoration of All Faithful Departed on November 2 is a recent addition to the calendar of the Episcopal Church in this country. It has, however, long had a place in some other Anglican calendars, and the history of this observance goes back many centuries. In medieval Catholic usage, November 1 was a joyful day celebrating all the heroes, leaders, and exemplars of Christian faith. November 2, or All Soul's Day, was a penitential occasion invoking God's mercy on the ordinary dead, the sinners, who might only hope to enter heaven after a lengthy punishment in purgatory. At the time of the Reformation, Protestants strongly opposed what they regarded as idolatrous honor given to the saints and what they felt was sacrilegious intercession in behalf of souls already rejected or accepted by God. As usual, the Anglican Church attempted to hold to a middle course. Anglicanism had not maintained the sharp medieval differentiations between the cannonized saints and other Christian souls. We have understood All Saints' Day as a celebration of the communion of saints in the broadest sense—the unity of all the holy people of God in this world and the next. In the original latin wording of the Apostles' Creed *sanctorum communio* means the *communion of holy people*, but it also means the *communion of holy things*, the unity of all who share Holy Baptism, Holy Communion, and the holy faith. Hence, All Saints' Day and the commemoration of all Christian souls have in fact been observed together in most parishes on November 1. The custom of reading the names of all parishioners or relatives and friends of parishioners who have died during the preceding twelve months was originally an All Souls' Day usage, but among us it has often comfortably situated itself on All Saints' Day, or the following Sunday.

In many congregations, the reality is that it is possible to get a goodly number of people to church on an occasional major holy day in mid-week, such as All Saints' Day. But it is not possible to get such a congregation on two successive weekdays. On the other hand, the second day, now recognized in our Church as a lesser holy day commemorating all the faithful departed, will be welcome in parishes and institutions having daily services. Lesser holy days may always be legitimately transferred to another open weekday within the same week. Some congregations may find it convenient in years when All Saints' Day comes early in the week, to commemorate all the departed in the latter part of the week. Others will do so the following Sunday when the observance of All Saints is continued. It must be remembered, however, that this Sunday (like all other Sundays) must be primarily a feast—mourning cannot set the tone of the service on the Lord's Day.

One advantage of a separate commemoration of all the departed on a weekday is that it provides the opportunity for a requiem celebration of the Eucharist outside the traumatic context of the recent death of a particular individual. Many Episcopalians have had little exposure to the Requiem Mass and would benefit from it. Today we so often think of the Eucharist in terms of thanksgiving, joy, and praise that we may forget that it is also concerned with suffering, tragedy, and death. We need to know that this sacrifice and sacrament is available for the latter as well as the former circumstances. There are other also times, in addition to funerals for specific individuals, when a requiem is suitable for a weekday Eucharist.

As to the actual celebration of a requiem, our new Prayer Book offers a wider variety of available Propers, page 202 or 253. The liturgy itself can proceed along the usual pattern of Rite I or II, inserting these Propers, special intercession (pages 480-81 or 497), Proper Preface (pages 349 or 382), and Proper postcommunion prayer (pages 482 or 498). Another option would be simply to follow the order of burial itself (pages 469-83 or 491-500) concluding with the responsory "Give rest, O Christ" and the dismissal. In these orders for burial the proper material is indicated at the proper point for the Eucharist. A very distinctive service can be celebrated, giving great emphasis to the major Christian teachings about death and resurrection. The amount of material is such, however, that it must be studied carefully beforehand in planning the service. It will also be noted that Burial I and Burial II differ not only in their respective use of traditional and contemporary language, but also in some of the actual contents of the material.

If a non-eucharistic service commemorating the departed is desired, one may use the Ministry of the Word from the burial rite, or one may insert appropriate Psalms, lessons, and prayers into Morning Prayer. For a sevice later in the day, the Order of Worship for the Evening provides a striking context within which to use suitable Psalms, lesson, *Nunc dimittis*, and appropriate prayers. Our hymnal offers many suitable hymns in the sections for Easter, for saints' days, and for the departed. Among the latter, the great Swahili hymn, Jesus, Son of Mary, Number 223, may be recited by the congregation at a weekday service if singing is not possible. If weather permits, churches which have an adjacent graveyard or columbarium may consider the option of an out-of-doors service at this time. One possibility is to have the Ministry of the Word amidst the graves, with the intercessions said in procession going around the area. If the Eucharist is to be celebrated, all can then return into the church for the remainder of the service.

In the traditional Anglicanism of the British Isles, the physical presence of the graves of former parishioners around the church, or even in the church, has always been an eloquent visible expression of the communion of the living and the dead. I recently had the genuine pleasure of going through a country churchyard in Virginia with a veteran parishioner who patted the gravestones with his hand and recounted some personal reminiscences and anecdotes about each person who had been buried there in the last sixty or seventy years. Most of us in America today are not fortunate enough to be able to live and die among our own kith and kin. Hence, it is important to find other ways of expressing the solidarity of the dead and the living. The Christian does not live or die alone, and the goal toward which we journey is the resurrection in that place when all tears are wiped away and all things will be made new in Christ.

VII

*Ministers of the Liturgy:
Ordained and Lay*

39:
Lay People
and Clergy at Ordinations

Ordinations no longer tend to be confined to cathedrals and a few larger parish churches. An increasing number of dioceses now schedule ordinations in the parish church from which the ordinand comes, or to which the new deacon or priest will be assigned. The major decisions about the service are, of course, the responsibility of the bishop, but the planning of details is usually left in part to the clergy and people of the parish. Thus, it is an exceptional opportunity for the parish worship committee to carry out a challenging and creative assignment. In some dioceses, furthermore, the diocesan liturgical commission advises both the bishop and local people in making plans. The same may be true when a new church is to be consecrated, or a new minister installed, or when some other special diocesan, regional, or deanery function is held in a parish church. Such opportunities for cooperation should be taken full advantage of. For members of a parish committee, it can be a great source of encouragement and stimulation to spend an hour or so with some specially informed member of the diocesan commission, talking, exchanging ideas, and looking over the facilities of their church. Both the parish and the diocese are enriched by this kind of give-and-take in thinking about liturgy.

For the local congregation as a whole, such occasions can also bring many new insights. Singing different kinds of music, seeing different styles of vestments, hearing a visiting preacher, experiencing the Peace as a real accolade, participating in the excitement of the entire event: all this brings to local people, clergy and laity alike, a wider vision of the dimensions of worship.

Too often in the past, an ordination has been viewed as a purely clerical affair. The candidates started as lay persons. At the rite of ordination they went up into the chancel into a crowd of clergy, and from this they emerged as clergy themselves, no longer members of the laity in the nave of the church. Needless to say, this is not what ordination is supposed to mean. It is true that a new deacon or a new priest is solemnly inducted into a new sacramental relationship with the bishop and with other deacons and priests. But this is only part of what ordination means. The bishop is not ordaining new priests and deacons simply to supply the existing clergy with a greater number of peers. On the contrary, the ordinands are being ordained to forward the work of the Church to people, to preach to people, to minister to people, to pray for people, to lead the worship of people, and to enable people to find fulfillment and salvation in the Body of Christ. An essential part of the ordination of deacons and priests is that they are being invested with a new sacramental relationship toward all members of the Church. The planning and arrangement of the rite of ordination should reflect this in outward and visible signs.

The placement of the ordaining bishop in a position close to and facing the congregation, as required in the rubrics of the Proposed Prayer Book (pages 524 and 536), is thus not simply for convenience or to satisfy public curiosity, but to express the relation of the congregation as a whole to what is happening. Similarly, the inclusion of lay persons as well as clergy among the presenters of candidates, the responses by the congregation, and the reading of the Old Testament Lesson and the Epistle by lay persons, are not intended as cheerful expressions of ecclesiastical democracy but rather are supposed to voice the authentic responsibility of the membership of the Church in bringing forward the most suitable candidates for holy orders. The same is true of the music offered by the choir, the decorations arranged by the altar guild, the ceremonial carried out by the servers, and all the other work and planning which people have carried out.

In our Anglican tradition, as in Catholic usage throughout history, "the ordained ministry" is not simply one undefined state of

religious activity. There are three distinct kinds of ordained ministers—bishops, priests, and deacons—and the carrying out of their
distinct roles greatly enhances the meaning and dramatic clarity of
the ordination rite. Consequently, if a deacon is available to read
the Gospel and perform other diaconal duties, these functions
should not be usurped by priests. It is often said that every priest
is still in a sense a deacon, but this is certainly not the thrust of the
liturgical rubrics which specify deacons at certain points. Similarly,
priests participating in an ordination should not default in their own
distinct presbyteral functions. To blur the two orders is to confuse
the clarity of whichever role is being conferred on the ordained.

Finally, in receiving Holy Communion at the end of the service,
clergy and laity alike receive the sacred pledge of their unity with
the Lord Christ and with one another in the fellowship of the Holy
Spirit. They express the state of being "in communion" with one
another in their several orders and vocations, and they solemnly
affirm their recognition and acceptance of the Eucharist which has
been carried out with the active participation and functioning of
the new deacon or new priest.

40:
Priestly Concelebration

When several priests are to be involved in the celebration of the Holy Eucharist, what should they do? This question often arises on special occasions when one or more visiting clergy come to a church. In large parishes, it may arise every week as duties are divided among the rector and the curates. This is partly a practical question involving the space for the convenient seating and movements of the clergy, the number of communicants to be served, the character and appearance of available vestments, and so forth. Yet it is also a theological question. As in the Eucharist we celebrate the Sacrament of the Lord's Body, so the assembled Church should be an outward sign of the Lord's Body, with different members carrying out different functions in an orderly and suitable manner. What different priests do will affect what a bishop or deacon will do, if either of these are present. It will affect what readers and servers do in the same service. It will also affect the experience and feeling of worship in the congregation as a whole. Good norms and patterns of procedure avoid the embarrassment and sloppiness of hasty last-minute decisions.

A hundred years ago, or even twenty years ago in many places, it was customary for an assisting clergyman, whether priest or deacon, only to read the Epistle and administer the chalice. If there were two assistants, one might read the Epistle and the other the Gospel. There was usually no convenient way to include a larger number of clergy in the action. Some places even followed the curious practice of having one priest read the entire service from beginning to end (including the Epistle and Gospel) even if several other clergy were present. The latter were permitted to assist only in the distribution of Holy Communion. Such an arrangement gave liturgical expression to a highly individualistic view of the priesthood.

A more corporate and collegial concept of the priesthood is expressed in the ancient and historically widespread custom of concelebration. This is the practice of having two or more priests stand together at the altar as an outward and visible expression of their partnership in the offering of the eucharistic sacrifice.

In 1956, the present author and some others published articles inviting the restoration of such a practice within the Episcopal Church. At that time, some greeted this proposal with consternation. Over the years, however, this usage gradually has come to be widely adopted at ordinations and other special occasions, and is a normal practice in some places where several clergy are regularly present. It has always been customary in Eastern Orthodoxy. It was widely revived within Roman Catholicism following Vatican Council II. It is especially appropriate at times when the bishop can officiate together with priests of his diocese. In a special sense, as the ancient liturgies said, they are his fellow presbyters and colleagues.

How is such a concelebration carried out? Usually the additional priests will wear surplices and stoles, or albs and stoles, or all may be fully vested in chasubles. If there are just two or three priests, they may share the entire service in a convenient manner. If there are more, it is suggested that the senior or chief celebrant officiate for the first part of the service. (This chief celebrant will, of course, be the bishop if he is present.) Before the *Sursum corda*, the others should come up to the altar and stand at the chief celebrant's right and left. During the eucharistic prayer, they should join together in the manual acts and other gestures (preferably made in a restrained and decorous manner). The breaking of the consecrated bread is an ancient function of the concelebrants. All can then make their Communions standing at the altar, passing the vessels from one to another.

In some places, the priests say part of the eucharistic prayer out loud. In the experience of the present writer, this tends to fracture the unity of the prayer, and destroys the dramatic similarity to the Last Supper. On the other hand, if a very long eucharistic prayer is used, such as Prayers I or D in the Proposed Book of Common Prayer, a good case can be made for having the chief celebrant sing or say the *Sursum corda* and first part of the canon, another priest say the oblation and invocation, and a third say the last part—or some similar division. Such an arrangement should be carefully planned in advance.

The concept of priestly concelebration is also applicable to some other rites as well as the Eucharist. At a baptism, if additional priests are present, it is appropriate for them to stand beside the chief celebrant at the font and extend their hands over the water which is to be blessed. As the Proposed Prayer Book suggests, different priests or deacons can then immerse or pour water over the candidates. Similarly, additional priests may extend their hands over the couple in the marriage blessing, or quite appropriately actually lay their hands on their heads.

Priestly concelebration is intended to augment corporate participation and to implement clearly the distinct functions of the priestly or presbyteral order. It should not, therefore, confuse or exclude the functioning of other orders. If one or more deacons are present, they certainly should carry on their distinct duties. Nor should the lay persons who read or serve be crowded out. Some lay people are embarrassed to go to the lectern to read the Epistle when the choir is full of clergy for some special occasion. Such modesty is commendable but misplaced. The Church could not exist without lay people. It is the group of clergy who should feel embarrassed to celebrate the Eucharist without active lay participation, the more so on special occasions when the full reality of the Church should be visibly expressed.

41:
Ordained Ministers in Liturgy and in Life

Persons interested in liturgy have generally encouraged a fuller restoration of the order of deacons. In part (but only in part), this has been because deacons make better liturgy. With a reasonable amount of planning, a second clergyman in the chancel with different vestments and a role distinctly different from that of the priest, almost inevitably brings about a more dramatic movement of the service. In traditional Christian liturgy, the role of the deacon has been understood not only to assist and help the presiding priest or bishop, but also to enhance and give solemnity to the rite as a whole.

At this point in the discussion, someone inevitably asks, "But what can a deacon do that a lay person can't do?" If this is a serious question, then it should be asked first of all at the top. "What can a bishop do that a lay person can't do?" What is the answer to that? An average bishop on an average day may get up, read Morning Prayer, eat breakfast, and go to his office to answer mail and receive calls. He may have a luncheon meeting with someone, and perhaps in the afternoon have one or more conferences or attend the meeting of a committee or board. If he is fortunate, he can spend the evening with his family. Instead, he may often have to spend the evening with the vestry of a troubled parish, or spend it on the road going to a place where he has an early engagement the next morning. Obviously, laymen can also do any of these things. In some particular cases, certain lay persons might do them better.

Does this mean that bishops are not doing what they are supposed to do? Far from it. A bishop is ordained and consecrated *primarily* to preach the Gospel and to unify, lead, and oversee the Church. He seeks to do these things by many means. Saying his prayers, leading an exemplary personal life, performing administrative duties, presiding at meetings, and talking with a great variety of people are some of the many things that he necessarily does as leader of the Church. It is because we have leaders consecrated in the apostolic succession that they are entrusted with the authoritative and sacred actions of baptism, eucharist, absolution, and other sacraments. The few unique functions of a bishop—to confirm, to consecrate chrism, to ordain, to consecrate new churches—these all belong to the bishop because he is the authoritative spokesman of the Church, not *vice versa.* After all, confirmation could be administered by priests, as in Eastern Orthodoxy. A handful of bishops would be quite sufficient to consecrate chrism, ordain priests and hallow the few new churches built each year by Anglicans in North America. Primarily each diocese employs a bishop not to do the unique things he alone can do sacramentally but to be a leader of the Church.

If we turn to the priesthood, it is true that we think of priests as being ordained primarily in order to administer sacraments. Yet historically, there is no doubt that a primary purpose of the ministers of this order is to serve as colleagues, associates, and councillors of the bishop in the governance of the diocese. Because priests are the bishop's ordained associates, they share with him in the privilege of baptizing, celebrating the Eucharist, and so forth.

What is a deacon really ordained for? This is a harder question. Bishops and priests are officers in the Church with responsibilities comparable to those of officers in all sorts of secular organizations. We can understand that. Deacons are different. Their role is a uniquely Christian one, with no exact secular counterpart. Their primary mandate, some of us believe, is to give sacramental embodiment to our Lord's teaching that the greatest shall be servant of all, and to lead the Church as a whole in implementing this teaching. To the secular world, this does not and cannot make sense. Even for us Christians, it is not easily understood. It is because the deacon serves, because he visits the poor, the aged, and the prisoners, because his ministry is uniquely associated with Jesus, that the deacon is the person especially suited to proclaim the words of Jesus in the Gospel, to pray for those in need, and to handle that cup of the New Covenant which is the sign of shared suffering and sacrifice.

In other words, the three ordained orders of the Church, the episcopate, the priesthood (or presbyterate), and the diaconate, all have traditional functions in the liturgy which express the reality of their active ministry in the Church and in the world. From a materialistic point of view, we could have a much more beautiful liturgy if it were carried out by a troupe of professional actors, with their trained knowledge of speech, posture, and gesture. Such artists do, indeed, have much to teach the Church about communication. The liturgy, however, is not a pageant or play to be acted out on a stage. It is to be worship in spirit and in truth. Those who take the leading roles must be carrying out real-life parts. What we do in church on Sunday morning is supposed to reflect our lives the rest of the week, and our daily lives are supposed to reflect our worship. This is true for every Christian. Part of the meaning of ordination however, is that the ordained minister is to reflect this in a direct, evident, and explicit way. When it ceases to be so, the reality of the liturgy is eroded, and it ceases to be believable. This topic may merit more thought than we usually give to it.

42:
More about Ordained Ministers

In the last essay we considered some of the principles underlying the liturgical functions of bishops, priests, and deacons. Let us pursue this further with a view to the application of these principles in parish churches.

The chief celebrant at the Holy Eucharist is responsible for leading, presiding, and giving continuity and order to the entire rite. The priest who is officiating should be clearly visible and audible. But he should not be so far separated from everyone else that worship appears to be something the priest is doing while everyone else is watching; nor something everyone else is doing while the priest is simply supervising. If an assistant clergyman or a lay cantor is leading the Litany, for instance, the priest should be praying like everyone else—not fidgeting about. If a reader is reading the Epistle, the priest should be setting an example of reverent and attentive listening—not shuffling through a hymnbook or sermon notes. Of course, there are times when a priest has misplaced his glasses or his notes, or suddenly needs a Kleenex, and an acolyte or server should be near enough so that a loud stage whisper is not necessary to summon assistance.

When it comes to a bishop, more of such personal assistance may be needed. When the bishop comes to your church once a year, he may not remember the arrangement in your sanctuary or recall what your acolytes have been taught to do or be familiar with the particular chants your congregation habitually sings. Besides, he may be tired after a long trip or puzzled by people whose names he is struggling to remember. The practice of having an attendant, or so-called chaplain, always at the bishop's side makes sense. So too does the old Anglican custom of having the rector or vicar of the local church begin the service and get it started in the way people are accustomed to. In any case, it is desirable for the bishop to save his energy for his sermon and the sacramental actions he is to perform. From the Offertory on, the bishop more easily takes over at the altar—especially if the local clergy have prepared the elements in suitable amounts at the Offertory, and later assist with the distribution and take care of the ablutions. As we have said before, it is appropriate for the bishop to invite the local priest or priests to stand beside him at the altar during the prayer of consecration, as a visible expression of the unity of the eucharistic ministry which belongs to the bishop and is shared by priests. It is always appropriate for a deacon or deacons to attend and assist the bishop, in addition to carrying out their own distinctive diaconal duties.

Should a deacon attend and assist a priest in this same way? I doubt it. Rectors and vicars do not usually need to be led about in their own chancels. The weekly liturgical leadership of the priest is, in this respect, different from the once-a-year appearance of the bishop. It demeans and distorts the diaconate for it to appear that the primary normal function of this order is to provide a guard of honor for priests. Some of the deacon's time is properly spent assisting the priest, but not most of it. There is much to be said for the Eastern Orthodox practice of having the deacon stationed during parts of the liturgy at a point midway between the altar and the people.

The role of deacons has been particularly problematical because, although the Church has had deacons since New Testament times, the average modern parish has not usually had one. Where it has, this has often been a young seminary graduate whose diaconate was regarded, by the deacon and others, as only a brief apprenticeship before ordination to the priesthood. In other cases, perpetual deacons have been used in small or remote congregations where the work was too difficult or the salary too small to command the services of a priest—this circumstance alone speaks volumes. We Episcopalians have not usually exposed ourselves to either the pastoral or the liturgical reality of the properly *normal* deacon, a man or woman ordained to a lifelong ministry of service in the path of Jesus Christ, outside of the professional, economic, social, and canonically privileged status of bishops and priests in the Church.

The present writer witnessed a pleasant change for the better when attending a clergy conference in the Diocese of Nevada. At the principal Eucharist, one deacon was crucifer, another gospeler, another led the intercessions. Together they arranged the elements on the altar at the Offertory, distributed Holy Communion, and made the ablutions. On this occasion, the bishop solemnized the twenty-fifth anniversary of his own ordination to the diaconate by renewing his own ordination vows and washing the feet of six representative persons in the diocese. It was a very striking service. In his sermon, the bishop voiced his hope that every congregation in the diocese might some day have its deacon.

What vestments are best for deacons? In some parishes they wear a dalmatic—a splendid garment very suitable for feasts. (In the earliest liturgical usage, there was no such thing as a penitential dalmatic, as it was not worn during penitential seasons.) A full traditional Anglican surplice is, of course, a liturgical vesture second to none in beauty, dignity, and practicality. A deacon looks especially well in a full-length deacon's stole, going under the right arm and over the left, with one end hanging down below the left knee in front, and the other end hanging down in back. The distinctive character of the deacon's dalmatic and stole can be preserved by having them worn only by persons serving in the diaconate.

What about albs with stoles worn over them? A beautifully made alb is a handsome garment and, unlike a surplice, spares the necessity for a cassock underneath. The ordinary commercial alb, on the other hand, is made for a priest to wear under a chasuble, and is scarcely attractive as an outer garment. An alb with a girdle, furthermore, strangely accentuates the bulges of middle age. Designers of vestments may consider the Eastern Orthodox usage of a deacon's alb that is ungirded and has orphreys on it much like a dalmatic. The stole is worn over it. In any case, parishes should think twice before investing in the type of High Mass set which includes a dalmatic for the gospeler and tunicle for the epistoler. Such a set implies that on all solemn occasions it will be precisely a priest, a deacon, and a subdeacon—no more and no less—who will be the principal ministers of the entire service. In most parishes, this does not conform to reality.

43:
Readers and Cantors

Those parts of the liturgy which come from the Bible, and which change from day to day and from week to week, are extremely important. They deserve our fullest care and attention. Deacons or priests reading the Gospel, and lay persons reading lessons or Epistles, will always do so more clearly and forcefully if they understand what they are reading and have in mind one or more things to be emphasized. This part of the liturgy will be improved if the clergy and lay people who read passages can sit down together and talk about what these passages mean. When readings come from one biblical book for a series of Sundays, the purpose and message of the entire book can be helpfully considered. Participation in such discussions will also help the choir leader or organist to find suitable hymns. In parishes which follow the very desirable practice of correlating the teaching in the Sunday school with the preaching in church, the Sunday school teachers will benefit by this same process. Taking the Bible readings seriously lays on the priest the obligation of preaching regularly about the passages which are read. There is often much to be said for basing a sermon on the Gospel, but a preacher should remember that if other people devote their time and effort to reading the Old Testament and the Epistle well, and if the whole congregation is expected to listen reverently to these various parts of the Bible, then the sermons should also allude to them in helpful and constructive ways. In fact, preachers will discover that the periodic discussion of the passages with lay readers and others will greatly assist them in choosing sermon topics that are of interest to their people.

It should be borne in mind, however, that such periodic discussions are a dangerous thing to start. The participants may very well become so interested that they will demand a regular ongoing adult class dealing with the books of the Bible that are read in the liturgy each year. Such a class presents a serious professional challenge to the clergy. Many, however, would feel that this is an extremely suitable and productive use of their time and energy. To teach the word of God is, after all, one of the basic functions for which they were ordained. In many congregations there is a lay person who is well able to undertake the responsibility for organizing such a group, arranging times of meeting, assigning topics to different persons to discuss, and so forth. Lessons, Epistles, and Gospels are not the only biblical material used in worship. Psalms and canticles are obviously important parts of Morning Prayer, but Episcopalians often forget their suitability for the Eucharist as well. The inclusion of psalms, Old Testament readings, and canticles in the first part of the Eucharist on a regular basis is one of the most important intentions of the eucharistic liturgy of the Proposed Book of Common Prayer. The use of a psalm between the Bible readings is indeed one of the oldest and most universal parts of the eucharistic liturgy. It can be announced immediately after the reading and the congregation can remain sitting. It may be recited either responsively, or antiphonally from one side to another, or it may be said in unison. Likewise, it may be sung in a variety of ways. In classical usage, *Gloria Patri* is not used with psalms which follow lessons. When three readings are used, a psalm may come after the Old Testament reading and a canticle after the Epistle. In this case, standing for the canticle would seem more appropriate.

A musical method of dealing with psalms and some of the canticles is responsorial chant. According to this very ancient and traditional method of psalmody, a cantor sings most of the material so that the congregation is only responsible for a small part which is repeated as a refrain or antiphon. Usually, the cantor begins with a refrain which all then repeat. The cantor proceeds with one or more verses and then all join in the refrain. The cantor goes on with more verses and the refrain follows in unison. And so to the end of the psalm or canticle, when the refrain is sung by all a final time. As will be seen, some skill, both in singing and in personal projection, is required of the cantor, but little strain is placed on the congregation, so that virtually any group of people can sing along with a good cantor.

Many of our choir directors and organists have not had experience with responsorial chanting, but they will find that a substantial literature exists with a variety of chants, some of remarkable beauty, both in the traditional plainsong style and in some more contemporary arrangements. Singers and musicians should be encouraged to inform themselves about psalmody through attendance at the various diocesan, regional, and ecumenical workshops on Church music which are regularly held in different parts of the country. Likewise, clergy need to be encouraged to allow the musical leadership to exercise the talents available.

At present, most of our parishes do not have within them an individual regularly identified as a cantor. Yet most congregations do have someone with the necessary voice and personality to fill this role. With training and practice the ability can be built up. In some cases three or four churches may group together to organize several training sessions. In many places our Roman Catholic or Lutheran neighbors can provide helpful professional expertise. The small financial investment required of the parish for this will be well worth it. Where two or more cantors can be had, a number of variations are possible—such as having two cantors alternate in singing successive verses of a psalm, or having one cantor lead the congregational refrains.

As with other things, if a congregation is not accustomed to singing or saying psalms or a variety of canticles, familiarity can be built up bit by bit. A single short psalm, for instance, can be used for several Sundays in succession until people know it and can enjoy it. Similarly, an appropriate canticle can be consistently used during a season of the year. On weekdays or at early celebrations on Sunday mornings, saying the psalms especially associated with Holy Communion, such as 16, 36, 43, or 63, will readily commend itself.

Why bother with psalms and canticles, especially when there are so many good hymns in the Hymnal? The answer is very simple. Hymns lend themselves to variety but psalms and canticles lend themselves to repetition, memorization, and deepening meaning over the years. The rhyme scheme and the sing-song meter of ordinary modern hymns lose their dignity with too-frequent repetition. Most metrical hymns furthermore are quite unsatisfactory for recitation without music. When recited, the words of many perfectly good hymns become mere doggerel. Biblical poetry, on the other hand, is quite different. Its irregular wording and its suggestive but sometimes puzzling phrases lend themselves to many moods and many occasions. When they have been used so often that worshipers know them well, they become a remarkable vehicle for Christian worship. Certainly, the conspicuous place given to psalms and canticles in Morning Prayer has been a major reason for the popular affection for this office. Those of us who recite the offices daily know how well the canticles wear after having been said literally thousands of times. There is no reason why this element of worship should stand in an either/or relationship to the sacramental devotion of the Eucharist. An adequate and catholic liturgy is one which gathers together all of the main strands of worship into a harmonious unity. This is the kind of comprehensive liturgy to which the Church should summon its people every Lord's Day.

Conclusion

44:
"Let Us Keep the Feast"

The Church Year begins in Advent and moves on through Christmas, Epiphany, Lent and Eastertide. The summer and autumn weeks then bring us on to All Saints' Day, Thanksgiving, and the Last Sunday after Pentecost, which in turn leads again to Advent, looking both to the end of all history, and to the recurrence of Christmas and the retelling of the "old, old story" of our salvation. Each stage leads on to the next, but each stage constantly points to the unchanging Good News and to that heavenly country toward which the people of God must always be moving.

On the one hand, the yearly repetition of the calendar is one of its most welcome features. As Hymn 135 says,

> Blessed feasts of blessed martyrs, Holy days of holy men, With affection's recollections Greet we your return again.

On the other hand, no two years are the same in any congregation. Christmas may or may not be on a weekend; Easter may be early or late, a new priest comes or an old one goes, new music may be learned. Pastoral needs change, and various events in the community call for Christian responses of various sorts. Each year offers opportunity for new insights, new expressions of Christian devotion, and new efforts on the part of people and clergy to express the age-old faith in prayer and praise. The Gospel tells us that the well-versed scribe can bring out of his treasury things old and new. (St. Matthew 13:52). Similarly, in these essays we have tried to suggest possibilities, resources, and options that are both old and new for enhancing the worship of Christian people week by week in their local congregations. Some of these are things that may commend themselves as part of the regular ongoing practice, to be greeted with affection each returning year.

The interplay between special feasts and fasts on the one hand and the regular routine of normal weeks on the other is a subtle matter with philosophic as well as theological overtones. It has been noted by historians that some peoples, in some times and places, favor great consistency. Others love the special days, the fiestas, the dramatic commemorations.

It seems to be characteristic of our Anglican brothers and sisters in England to stress the consistent. They have fought wars to enforce the uniform use of one rigid Book of Common Prayer in the British Isles. In the historic editions of the English Book of Common Prayer, morever, there was great consistency from week to week. Apart from the psalms and Bible readings, little changed from week to week or from season to season, as Morning Prayer, Litany, Holy Communion, and Evensong were performed with unvarying imperturbability.

American church people typically enjoy more variety. We like our Lent to be very penitential, and our Eastertide to be very festive. We love the Midnight Mass of Christmas and we are learning to love the Great Vigil of Easter. It would seem that we can express our own native liturgical instincts most fully in the variety of times and seasons—always remembering, however, that variety loses its interest if there is no norm, no consistency, with which the variations can interact. In responding to the different themes of different days and seasons, we are fortunate that large numbers of our people —old, young, and middle-aged—have many talents and creative abilities. These involve literary, dramatic, and musical ability, and plastic and visual artistry. They also involve skills in planning, organizing, and arranging. Some people in some parishes have talents which are well known and recognized. Others have talents which no one has yet noticed or nurtured. What a great day it will be when people think of our churches as places where good talents and abilities of all sorts are welcomed and developed! What a glorious sign of the coming of God's kingdom that will be!

We all know that most of the greatest works of architectural art all over the world have been temples, shrines, churches, and cathedrals. Much of the world's greatest music has been religious. Many of the old masters' paintings are altarpieces. All the world admires these compositions. Perhaps, however, it brings just as much joy to the angels in heaven when a small volunteer choir does their best to master a new hymn for a special day, or when someone makes a bold new paschal candleholder in his workshop, or when a group of women construct a Lenten array and get it successfully mounted in time for Ash Wednesday, or when a local student makes original designs for the Sunday mimeographed bulletin, or when a large lamb-cake (complete with wool of shredded coconut) is baked for consumption after the Great Vigil on the Queen of Feasts!

These things will not be put in museums for later generations to stare at: they will be used here and now, on the days for which they are intended, and offered up to God's glory. The things that are typical of feasts—candles, flowers, music, new clothes, food and drink, processions and parades—these are all things that last for a day. The feast that does not end is above, where Jerusalem is adorned as a bride for her husband, and the song of Alleluia never ceases.

Index